D0553412

500

juices & smoothies

500
juices & smoothies

Christine Watson

A Quintet Book

First published in the UK in 2008 by
Apple Press
74-77 White Lion Street
London N1 9PF

www.apple-press.com

ISBN: 978-1-84543-261-4
QTT.LSMO

This book was conceived, designed, and produced by
Quintet Publishing Limited
4th Floor, Sheridan House
114-116 Western Road
Hove, East Sussex
BN3 1DD
United Kingdom

Managing Editor: Donna Gregory
Editorial Assistant: Robert Davies
Proofreader: Diana Chambers
Indexer: Dorothy Frame
Designer: Dean Martin
Art Director: Sofia Henry
Photography: Ian Garlick
Publisher: Gillian Laskier

20 19 18 17 16 15 14 13 12 11

Printed in China by 1010 Printing International Ltd.

contents

introduction

We are all constantly reminded that we don't get enough fruit or vegetables into our diets and for most of us, it's true. There is sufficient evidence that shows us that people can beat illness, fight cancers, lose weight, have better skin and hair and are generally healthier if they eat a large variety of fruit and vegetables every day.

Our bodies need fresh foods. The human body doesn't deal well with the processed food that saturates our supermarkets these days, and more and more people are beginning to realise this. Unfortunately, though, with our busy lifestyles, it can be hard to fill our bodies with what they need.

Juices and smoothies offer a surprisingly varied way of getting our fill. An 8-ounce glass of juice or smoothie can be a way of getting 4 or even 5 of our daily fruit or vegetable portions into our system. A smoothie is portable and you can drink it on the go, meaning there are no excuses for missing breakfast again. Making juices and smoothies is a great way of using up fruit or vegetables that are beginning to go past their best. Some of these recipes can even be eaten as desserts.

With a selection of creamy milkshakes, indulgent naughty but nice drinks and even some boozy blends, there is a blended drink here to suit everyone and every occasion.

But let's not forget that the most important benefit of anything we eat or drink is pleasure, and there is little better than drinking the nectar of sweet fragrant fruits. Have you ever drunk the juice of freshly pressed apples? Let me tell you that there is nothing sweeter. It is everything that an apple is: crisp, dry and sweet, but where apples can be hard to digest as a fruit, they glide down easily as a juice. Delicious!

equipment

blenders or smoothie makers

It is so important to get a good quality blender when making a smoothie. Try to find one that has an ice-crushing setting on it, as this will help you make frozen cocktails or thick and frosty drinks. Smoothie makers are a fun concept and do the job well, but are a bit of a gimmick and standard blenders often have more power. Hand blenders can work for the simpler fruit smoothies but will be no match for the icy ones.

centrifugal juice extractors

Juice extractors come in various qualities and styles, but the best you can get is a professional-standard centrifugal juicer. They make a finer juice and remove more pulp, but get the best out of the fruit or vegetables that you put through them. The cheaper compact juicers are great for people on a budget, but if you think you're going to be serious about juicing, I would suggest spending the money on a better quality one.

citrus juicer

Even though you can juice citrus fruit in a centrifugal juicer if you peel it, it is important to have a citrus juicer on hand for when you only need a little bit of citrus juice and don't need to use the larger equipment.

lidded glasses and portable cups

A lidded glass or portable cup can be stored in the fridge to keep any juice or smoothie you can't drink, or you could use it to carry a freshly made smoothie to work with you.

resealable plastic bags

Chop up your fruit the night before and pop it in the freezer in a resealable plastic bag. The next day put the frozen fruit straight into the blender with some yogurt or juice and blitz for an icy smooth drink.

measuring spoons

By using measuring spoons you are guaranteed to get the right amount of each ingredient into your drink, making sure you get the flavour perfectly balanced.

ice cream scoop

It is good to have an ice cream scoop on hand to make it easier to scoop ice cream or frozen yogurt for the frostier drinks.

ingredients

fresh fruit and vegetables
Fruits and vegetables that are available to you seasonally will taste best, but pretty much all fruits and vegetables can be juiced.

frozen fruit
Ready-frozen fruit is great if something you want is out of season. Either defrost them when making juices or use them frozen for making smoothies.

dried fruits
Dried fruits are great in smoothies and some milkshakes, but make sure they are not too dry. If they are, soak them in some water, juice or alcohol for a few minutes before using.

canned fruit
As with frozen fruit, some canned fruits are great as an alternative to expensive fruits like lychees or out-of-season fruits like apricots, although the real thing will always make the best drinks.

yoghurt
Greek yoghurt is the mildest and creamiest of all the yoghurts and I feel it makes the best smoothie, but flavour is a matter of taste, so use whichever yoghurt you like best. Vegans can use non-dairy yoghurt and enjoy any of the recipes in this book.

bottled juices
For those of you with little time, it's a good cheat to have a bottle of freshly squeezed orange or apple juice in the fridge.

ice cream and frozen yoghurt

A simple vanilla ice cream or plain frozen yoghurt is a great base for most milkshakes or frozen smoothies, but do play around with some of the amazing flavours you can get these days, such as ginger and white chocolate, to make some really exciting drinks. Soya ice cream and frozen yoghurt are widely available, meaning that those who avoid dairy products can still enjoy a thick and creamy smoothie.

ice

A well-stocked ice compartment in your freezer is essential when making any drinks, especially the frozen cocktails and thick, icy shakes in this book.

sugar syrup

You will need this when making some of the alcoholic cocktails in the last chapter; to prepare it, simply stir 450 g (1 lb) sugar into 475 ml (16 fl oz) water and place in a pan over a low heat. Stir until the sugar is dissolved, bring to the boil and boil rapidly for 4 minutes. Leave to cool, then place in a sealed container in the refrigerator and use as needed.

alcohols

Whether it be rum, vodka or tequila that's your drink of choice, you will find a fruity blend to go with it. Feel free to mix a couple of tablespoons of alcohol into any of the drinks in this book – you may discover your new favourite party drink.

simple
smoothies

Smoothies are sweet, blended drinks made from

fresh fruit. The possible permutations of fruit are

endless and this chapter will inspire you to try

dozens of them. Fruit doesn't have to be the only

ingredient – some of these recipes include milk

or yoghurt to thicken the drink and make it

more filling.

peach and raspberry smoothie

see variations page 32

This classic combination relies on the sweetness of a ripe peach to work well – but be sure the peach is not overripe, or it will have an unpleasant taste.

1 peach, stoned and quartered
75 g (2³/₄ oz) raspberries
120 ml (4 fl oz) plain low-fat yoghurt
120 ml (4 fl oz) milk

Put all the ingredients in a blender. Blend for 1 minute or until smooth. Pour into a glass and serve immediately.

Serves 1

banana and strawberry smoothie

see variations page 33

This is a seriously rich yet healthy smoothie that has become a classic because the sweet flavours of banana and strawberry are perfectly complementary.

1 banana, peeled and quartered
150 g (5¹/₂ oz) strawberries, hulled
120 ml (4 fl oz) plain low-fat yoghurt
60 ml (2 fl oz) milk

Put all the ingredients in a blender. Blend for 1 minute or until smooth. Pour into a glass and serve immediately.

Serves 1

strawberry and apricot smoothie

see variations page 34

This smoothie slips down with no problem at all. It is one of those classic combinations that cannot fail to please.

75 g (2³/₄ oz) strawberries, hulled
2 apricots, halved and stoned
120 ml (4 fl oz) plain low-fat yoghurt
60 ml (2 fl oz) milk
1 tsp honey (optional)

Put all the ingredients in a blender. Blend for 1 minute or until smooth. Pour into a glass and serve immediately.

Serves 1

plum and passion fruit smoothie

see variations page 35

This combination makes a deliciously creamy smoothie with a wonderful colour.

3 red or purple plums, halved and stoned
Pulp of 2 passion fruit, sieved
120 ml (4 fl oz) plain low-fat yoghurt
60 ml (2 fl oz) milk

Put all the ingredients in a blender. Blend for 1 minute or until smooth. Pour into a glass and serve immediately.

Serves 1

mango and passion fruit smoothie

see variations page 36

The astringent flavour of passion fruit cuts through the rich sweetness of mango, lightening the effect of this aromatic smoothie.

1 medium mango, peeled, stoned and cut into chunks
Pulp of 2 passion fruit
120 ml (4 fl oz) plain low-fat yoghurt
120 ml (4 fl oz) milk

Put all the ingredients in a blender. Blend for 1 minute or until smooth. Pour into a glass. Sprinkle a few passion fruit seeds over the top of the smoothie if desired and serve immediately.

Serves 1

blackberry and raspberry smoothie

see variations page 37

The deep purple colour of this smoothie is picture-perfect.

150 g (5¹/₂ oz) blackberries
75 g (2³/₄ oz) raspberries
120 ml (4 fl oz) plain low-fat yoghurt
60 ml (2 fl oz) milk
1 tsp honey (optional)

Put all the ingredients in a blender. Blend for 1 minute or until smooth. Pour into a glass and serve immediately.

Serves 1

blueberry and strawberry smoothie

see variations page 38

Take advantage of the fresh wild blueberries available in late summer if you can.

75 g (2³/₄ oz) blueberries
150g (5¹/₂ oz) strawberries, hulled
120 ml (4 fl oz) plain low-fat yoghurt
60ml (2 fl oz) milk

Put all the ingredients in a blender. Blend for 1 minute or until smooth. Pour into a glass and serve immediately.

Serves 1

papaya and mango smoothie

see variations page 39

A thick and sustaining smoothie, but delicately fragrant with the scents of tropical fruits.

100 g (3¹/₂ oz) peeled papaya chunks
100 g (3¹/₂ oz) peeled mango chunks
120 ml (4 fl oz) plain low-fat yoghurt
60 ml (2 fl oz) milk

Put all the ingredients in a blender. Blend for 1 minute or until smooth. Pour into a glass and serve immediately.

Serves 1

melon and kiwi fruit smoothie

see variations page 40

The vivid green of this drink is as refreshing as its vibrant sweetness.

100 g (3½ oz) honeydew melon chunks
2 kiwi fruit, peeled
120 ml (4 fl oz) plain low-fat yoghurt
60 ml (2 fl oz) milk

Put all the ingredients in a blender. Blend for 1 minute or until smooth. Pour into a glass and serve immediately.

Serves 1

blackberry and blackcurrant smoothie

see variations page 41

The classic woodland flavours make this the perfect autumn smoothie.

150 g (5¹/₂ oz) blackberries
75 g (3¹/₂ oz) blackcurrants
120 ml (4 fl oz) plain low-fat yoghurt
60 ml (2 fl oz) milk

Put all the ingredients in a blender. Blend for 1 minute or until smooth. Pour into a glass and serve immediately.

Serves 1

variations

peach and raspberry smoothie

see base recipe page 15

peach, raspberry and mint smoothie

Prepare the basic recipe, adding a few fresh mint leaves to the blend.

peach and orange smoothie

Prepare the basic recipe, replacing the raspberries and milk with
180 ml (6 fl oz) orange juice.

raspberry and orange smoothie

Prepare the basic recipe, but omit the peach and milk, increase the
quantity of raspberries to 150 g (5½ oz) and add 120 ml (4 fl oz)
orange juice to the blend.

peach, raspberry and orange smoothie

Prepare the basic recipe, omitting the milk and replacing it with 60 ml
(2 fl oz) orange juice.

variations

banana and strawberry smoothie

see base recipe page 17

banana, strawberry and orange smoothie
Prepare the basic recipe, replacing the milk with 60 ml (2 fl oz) orange juice.

strawberry and orange smoothie
Prepare the basic recipe, omitting the milk and banana, adding 60 ml
(2 fl oz) orange juice and increasing the strawberries to 200 g (7 oz).

strawberry smoothie
Prepare the basic recipe, omitting the banana and increasing the quantity of
strawberries to 200 g (7 oz).

banana and raspberry smoothie
Prepare the basic recipe, omitting the strawberries and replacing them with
the same quantity of raspberries.

strawberry and apricot smoothie

see base recipe page 18

raspberry and apricot smoothie
Prepare the basic recipe, omitting the strawberries and replacing them with the same quantity of raspberries.

strawberry, apricot and orange smoothie
Prepare the basic recipe, omitting the milk and replacing it with the same quantity of orange juice.

strawberry, apricot and apple smoothie
Prepare the basic recipe, omitting the milk and replacing it with the same quantity of apple juice.

strawberry, peach and apple smoothie
Prepare the basic recipe, omitting the milk and apricots and replacing them with 60 ml (2 fl oz) apple juice and 1 stoned and quartered peach.

plum and passion fruit smoothie

see base recipe page 21

plum, passion fruit and orange smoothie
Prepare the basic recipe, omitting the milk and replacing it with the same quantity of orange juice.

plum smoothie
Prepare the basic recipe but omit the passion fruit.

plum, passion fruit and apple smoothie
Prepare the basic recipe, omitting the milk and replacing it with the same quantity of apple juice.

plum and orange smoothie
Prepare the basic recipe, omitting the milk and replacing it with the same quantity of orange juice. Omit the passion fruit also.

plum and rhubarb smoothie
Prepare the basic recipe, omitting the passion fruit and replacing it with 50 g (1³/₄ oz) stewed rhubarb.

variations

mango and passion fruit smoothie

see base recipe page 22

mango, passion fruit and lime smoothie
Prepare the basic recipe, adding a squeeze of lime juice to the blend.

mango, passion fruit and orange smoothie
Prepare the basic recipe, omitting the milk and replacing it with the same quantity of orange juice.

mango, passion fruit and pineapple smoothie
Prepare the basic recipe, omitting the milk and replacing it with the same quantity of pineapple juice.

mango, passion fruit, orange and pineapple smoothie
Prepare the basic recipe, omitting the milk and replacing it with 1 tablespoon orange juice and 2 tablespoons pineapple juice.

mango, passion fruit and rose water smoothie
Prepare the basic recipe, adding $1/2$ teaspoon rose water to the other ingredients.

blackberry and raspberry smoothie

see base recipe page 25

blackberry smoothie
Prepare the basic recipe, omitting the raspberries and increasing the quantity of blackberries to 225 g (8 oz).

raspberry smoothie
Prepare the basic recipe, omitting the blackberries and increasing the quantity of raspberries to 225 g (8 oz).

blackberry and orange smoothie
Prepare the basic recipe, omitting the raspberries and milk, and replacing them with 225 g (8 oz) blackberries and 60 ml (2 fl oz) orange juice.

raspberry and orange smoothie
Prepare the basic recipe, omitting the blackberries and milk, and replacing them with 225 g (8 oz) raspberries and 60 ml (2 fl oz) orange juice.

variations

blueberry and strawberry smoothie

see base recipe page 26

blueberry, strawberry and orange smoothie

Prepare the basic recipe, omitting the milk and replacing it with the same quantity of orange juice.

blueberry, strawberry and apple smoothie

Prepare the basic recipe, omitting the milk and replacing it with the same quantity of apple juice.

blueberry, strawberry and pineapple smoothie

Prepare the basic recipe, omitting the milk and replacing it with the same quantity of pineapple juice.

blueberry, raspberry and apple smoothie

Prepare the basic recipe, omitting the milk and strawberries, and replacing them with 60 ml (2 fl oz) apple juice and 150 g (5$\frac{1}{2}$ oz) raspberries.

papaya and mango smoothie

see base recipe page 28

papaya smoothie
Prepare the basic recipe, omitting the mango and replacing it with an extra
100g (3½ oz) papaya.

papaya and lime smoothie
Prepare the basic recipe, omitting the mango and replacing it with an extra
100g (3½ oz) papaya and a squeeze of lime juice.

mango, papaya and orange smoothie
Prepare the basic recipe, omitting the milk and replacing it with the same
quantity of orange juice.

mango, papaya and pineapple smoothie
Prepare the basic recipe, omitting the milk and replacing it with the same
quantity of pineapple juice.

variations

melon and kiwi fruit smoothie

see base recipe page 29

melon, kiwi fruit and apple smoothie
Prepare the basic recipe, omitting the milk and replacing it with the same quantity of apple juice.

melon, kiwi fruit and orange smoothie
Prepare the basic recipe, omitting the milk and replacing it with the same quantity of orange juice.

melon, kiwi fruit and pineapple smoothie
Prepare the basic recipe, omitting the milk and replacing it with the same quantity of pineapple juice.

kiwi fruit smoothie
Prepare the basic recipe, omitting the melon and adding 1 extra kiwi fruit.

variations

blackberry and blackcurrant smoothie

see base recipe page 31

blackberry, blackcurrant and orange smoothie

Prepare the basic recipe, omitting the milk and replacing it with the same quantity of orange juice.

blackberry, blackcurrant and apple smoothie

Prepare the basic recipe, omitting the milk and replacing it with the same quantity of apple juice.

blackberry and blueberry smoothie

Prepare the basic recipe, omitting the blackcurrants and replacing them with 75 g (2³/₄ oz) blueberries.

blackberry and apple smoothie

Prepare the basic recipe, omitting the blackcurrants and milk, and replacing them with an extra 75 g (2³/₄ oz) blackberries and 60 ml (2 fl oz) apple juice.

breakfast blends

A thick and fruity smoothie is perfect for breakfast.

Substantial, filling and healthy, these are meals in a

glass and a perfect start to your day.

apricot breakfast smoothie

see variations page 60

The oats in this breakfast smoothie provide a slow release of energy throughout the morning, helping to keep you satisfied until lunch. The oats also add a creamy texture to the smoothie.

3 apricots, halved and stoned
180 ml (6 fl oz) apple juice
180 ml (6 fl oz) plain low-fat yoghurt
1 tsp honey
1 tbsp rolled oats

Place all the ingredients into a blender and blend for 1 minute. Pour into a glass and serve immediately.

Serves 1

blueberry, raspberry, peach and orange smoothie

see variations page 61

This delicious wake-up combination will have you wanting to set your alarm just that little bit earlier.

35 g (1¼ oz) blueberries
35 g (1¼ oz) raspberries
1 peach, halved and stoned
120 ml (4 fl oz) orange juice
180 ml (6 fl oz) plain low-fat yoghurt
2 tsp honey

Place all the ingredients into a food blender and blend for 1 minute. Pour into a glass and serve immediately.

Serves 1

banana, peach and strawberry smoothie

see variations page 62

During the summer months try putting the fruit into the freezer the night before you make this smoothie. This ensures it is really cold and refreshing by breakfast time.

1 banana, peeled and quartered
1 peach, halved and stoned
4 strawberries, hulled
180 ml (6 fl oz) orange juice
1 tsp honey

Place all the ingredients into a blender and blend for 1 minute. Pour into a glass and serve immediately.

Serves 1

carnival smoothie

see variations page 63

As the name suggests, this smoothie has a Caribbean flavour. It's sure to perk up your morning routine.

Pulp and juice of 1 passion fruit (sieve if preferred)
1½ mangoes, peeled, stoned and diced
240 ml (8 fl oz) pineapple juice
1 banana, peeled and quartered
2 Brazil nuts

Place all the ingredients into a blender and blend for 1 minute. Pour into a glass and serve immediately. Garnish with a piece of fresh pineapple if desired.

Serves 1

go bananas smoothie

see variations page 64

A thick and filling smoothie to set you up for a day at the office.

1½ bananas, peeled and quartered
1 tbsp smooth peanut butter
240 ml (8 fl oz) milk

Place all the ingredients into a blender and blend for 1 minute. Pour into a glass and serve immediately.

Serves 1

wake-up juice

see variations page 65

The zesty flavours of this citrus combination are guaranteed to kick-start your day as well as your taste buds.

2 grapefruit, peeled
2 oranges, peeled
1 lemon, peeled

Put all the ingredients through a juice extractor. Pour into a glass and serve immediately. You can also make this juice in a citrus juicer wih halved fruits.

Serves 1

apple and orange juice

see variations page 66

This is perhaps the most traditional and familiar of all fruit juice combinations – and with good reason.

3 whole apples
3 oranges, peeled

Put the apples and oranges through a juice extractor. Pour into a glass and serve immediately.

Serves 1

nectarine and raspberry juice

see variations page 67

The sunny flavour of this juice is a perfect remedy for days when the weather is anything but tropical.

3 nectarines, halved and stoned
150 g (5½ oz) raspberries

Put the nectarines and raspberries through a juice extractor. Pour into a glass and serve immediately.

Serves 1

mocha breakfast smoothie

see variations page 68

A caffeine pick-me-up softened with the smooth, rich flavour of cocoa. Try warming the milk gently for extra comfort.

1 banana, peeled and quartered
1 tbsp cocoa powder
2 tbsp (1 shot) espresso
240 ml (8 fl oz) milk (cold or hot)

Place all the ingredients into a blender. Blend for 1 minute or until smooth. Pour into a glass or coffee mug and serve immediately.

Serves 1

country breakfast smoothie

see variations page 69

Using stewed fruit is a novel approach to smoothie making, but this fruit adds a mellow
flavour that you don't get from fresh fruits.

1 apple
1 pear
200g (7 oz) chopped rhubarb
35 g (1¼ oz) blackberries
Squeeze of lemon juice
1 tsp honey
120 ml (4 fl oz) plain low-fat yoghurt

Peel, core and chop the apple and pear. Place all of the fruits into a saucepan with
2 tablespoons water, the lemon juice and the honey. Bring to the boil, then turn down to
a simmer. Poach the fruit for 10 minutes or until it is tender. Remove from the heat and
let it cool. Place the stewed fruit into a blender with the yoghurt. Blend for 1 minute or
until smooth. Pour into a glass and serve immediately. Drizzle a little extra honey over the
smoothie if desired.

Serves 1

variations

apricot breakfast smoothie

see base recipe page 43

peach and banana breakfast smoothie

Prepare the basic recipe, omitting the apricots and replacing them with 1 peach and ½ banana.

blueberry breakfast smoothie

Prepare the basic recipe, omitting the apricots and replacing them with 150 g (5½ oz) blueberries.

apricot and wheatgerm breakfast smoothie

Prepare the basic recipe, omitting the rolled oats and replacing them with 1 tablespoon wheatgerm.

apricot and strawberry breakfast smoothie

Prepare the basic recipe, omitting 1 apricot and replacing it with 4 hulled strawberries.

variations

blueberry, raspberry, peach and orange smoothie

see base recipe page 44

blueberry and orange smoothie
Prepare the basic recipe, omitting the raspberries and peach, and increasing the quantity of blueberries to 150 g (5½ oz).

blueberry and peach smoothie
Prepare the basic recipe, omitting the raspberries and increasing the quantity of blueberries to 75 g (2¾ oz) and the peach to 1½ halved and stoned peaches.

raspberry, apricot and orange smoothie
Prepare the basic recipe, omitting the blueberries and peach, and replacing them with 3 halved and stoned apricots.

blueberry, raspberry, peach and apple smoothie
Prepare the basic recipe, omitting the orange juice and replacing it with the same quantity of apple juice.

variations

banana, peach and strawberry smoothie

see base recipe page 47

banana and peach smoothie
Prepare the basic recipe, omitting the strawberries and adding an additional halved and stoned peach.

banana, peach and strawberry yoghurt smoothie
Prepare the basic recipe, omitting 60 ml (2 fl oz) orange juice and replacing it with 60 ml (2 fl oz) plain low-fat yoghurt.

banana, apricot and strawberry smoothie
Prepare the basic recipe, omitting the peach and replacing it with 2 halved and stoned apricots.

banana, peach and blackberry smoothie
Prepare the basic recipe, omitting the strawberries and replacing them with 35 g (1¼ oz) blackberries.

variations

carnival smoothie

see base recipe page 48

passion fruit and mango smoothie
Prepare the basic recipe, omitting the Brazil nuts and banana, and increasing the quantity of passion fruit to 2 fruits.

australian smoothie
Prepare the basic recipe, replacing the Brazil nuts with 5 macadamia nuts.

tropical smoothie
Prepare the basic recipe, omitting the Brazil nuts.

papaya and passion fruit smoothie
Prepare the basic recipe, omitting the Brazil nuts and chopped mango, and replacing them with ½ deseeded and chopped papaya and a squeeze of lime juice.

mixed nuts carnival smoothie
Prepare the basic recipe, adding 4 walnut halves and 3 blanched almonds to the other ingredients.

variations

go bananas smoothie

see base recipe page 51

go wheat and bananas
Prepare the basic recipe, adding 1 teaspoon of wheatgerm to the blender along with the other ingredients.

go bran and bananas
Prepare the basic recipe, adding 1 teaspoon of bran to the blender along with the other ingredients.

soy go bananas
Prepare the basic recipe, replacing the milk with the same quantity of soya milk.

go nuts and bananas
Prepare the basic recipe, adding 1 tablespoon of your favourite nuts to the blender along with the other ingredients.

go bananas and chocolate
Prepare the basic recipe, adding 1 tablespoon chocolate spread to the blender along with the other ingredients.

variations

wake-up juice

see base recipe page 52

rose water wake-up juice
Prepare the basic recipe. When you have poured the juice into a glass, add
1 teaspoon rose water and stir well to mix.

orange flower water wake-up juice
Prepare the basic recipe. When you have poured the juice into a glass, add
1 teaspoon orange flower water and stir well to mix.

ginger wake-up juice
Prepare the basic recipe, adding a 2-cm (³/₄-inch) chunk of peeled root
ginger to the ingredients before passing them through the juice extractor.

ginger and chilli wake-up juice
Prepare the basic recipe, adding a 2-cm (³/₄-inch) chunk of peeled root
ginger and 1/2 a deseeded red chilli to the ingredients before passing them
through the juice extractor.

mint wake-up juice
Prepare the basic recipe, adding 6 fresh mint leaves to the ingredients before
passing them through the juice extractor.

variations

apple and orange juice

see base recipe page 54

pear and orange juice
Prepare the basic recipe, omitting the apples and replacing them with
3 pears.

pineapple and orange juice
Prepare the basic recipe, omitting the apples and replacing them with
225 g (8 oz) peeled pineapple chunks.

pineapple and apple juice
Prepare the basic recipe, omitting the oranges and replacing them with
225 g (8 oz) peeled pineapple chunks.

pineapple and pear juice
Prepare the basic recipe, omitting the oranges and apples and replacing
them with 225 g (8 oz) peeled pineapple chunks and 2 pears.

variations

nectarine and raspberry juice

see base recipe page 55

nectarine and strawberry juice
Prepare the basic recipe, omitting the raspberries and replacing them with
5 hulled strawberries.

nectarine and blackberry juice
Prepare the basic recipe, omitting the raspberries and replacing them with
150 g (5½ oz) blackberries.

nectarine and blueberry juice
Prepare the basic recipe, omitting the raspberries and replacing them with
150 g (5½ oz) blueberries.

nectarine and plum juice
Prepare the basic recipe, omitting the raspberries and replacing them with
3 halved and stoned purple plums.

nectarine and apricot juice
Prepare the basic recipe, omitting the raspberries and replacing them with
2 halved and stoned apricots.

variations

mocha breakfast smoothie

see base recipe page 56

coffee breakfast smoothie
Prepare the basic recipe, omitting the cocoa powder.

cappuccino breakfast smoothie
Prepare the basic recipe, omitting the cocoa powder. When serving, sprinkle the top of the glass with cocoa powder.

rich mocha breakfast smoothie
Prepare the basic recipe, adding 2 tablespoons double cream to the ingredients before blending.

double shot mocha breakfast smoothie
Prepare the basic recipe, adding another shot (2 tablespoons) of espresso to the ingredients before blending.

chocolate orange breakfast smoothie
Prepare the basic recipe, omitting the espresso shot and replacing it with 1 tablespoon rind-free marmalade, thinned down with 1 tablespoon hot water.

variations

country breakfast smoothie

see base recipe page 59

spiced country smoothie
Prepare the basic recipe, adding 1 teaspoon mixed spice to the stewed fruit before blending.

stewed rhubarb, apple and pear smoothie
Prepare the basic recipe, omitting the blackberries.

stewed apple and blackberry smoothie
Prepare the basic recipe, omitting the rhubarb and pears, and replacing them with another apple and an additional 115 g (4 oz) blackberries.

stewed pear and apple smoothie
Prepare the basic recipe, omitting the rhubarb and blackberries, and replacing them with an additional ½ apple and ½ pear.

fragrant infusions

Adding aromatic ingredients to your smoothies and juices makes them even more seductive. Try cardamom or lemongrass for a taste of the Orient, or orange flower water or mint for an authentic flavour of the Middle East. This chapter is full of fragrant inspiration.

mandarin, lemongrass, chilli and mint juice

see variations page 88

Adding chilli to fruit juice might sound bizarre – but in small quantities it provides a flavour hit without excessive heat.

4 mandarin oranges, peeled
1 lemongrass stalk, trimmed
$^1/_2$ a long red chilli, deseeded
5 fresh mint leaves

Put all the ingredients through a juice extractor. Pour into a glass and serve immediately.

Serves 1

lychee, raspberry and rose water fizz

see variations page 89

The delicate scent of rose water adds an even more exotic note to the unusual combination of lychees and raspberries.

300 g (10¹/₂ oz) peeled and stoned lychees
150 g (5¹/₂ oz) raspberries
1 tsp rose water
120 ml (4 fl oz) sparkling water

Put the lychees and raspberries through a juice extractor. Stir in the rose water. Pour into a glass, top with sparkling water and serve immediately.

Serves 1

mango, coconut and lime smoothie

see variations page 90

The addition of lime brings a necessary edge to the creamy blend of coconut and mango.

1 mango, peeled and stoned
60 ml (2 fl oz) coconut cream
Juice of 1 lime
240 ml (8 fl oz) ice cubes

Place all the ingredients into a blender and blend for 1 minute or until smooth. Pour into a glass and serve immediately.

Serves 1

pineapple, lemongrass and cardamom crush

see variations page 91

Cardamom is most familiar in Western kitchens as a spice used in curries and Asian-style dishes. Yet in south Asia and the Middle East, it is commonly used in sweet preparations too – and it works wonderfully as a warm aromatic in Asian-flavoured juices like this one.

½ pineapple, peeled
1 lemongrass stalk, trimmed
Seeds from 2 cardamom pods
Juice of ½ lime

Put the pineapple and lemongrass through a juice extractor. Pour into a blender with the cardamom seeds and lime juice, and blend for 30 seconds. Pour into a glass and serve immediately.

Serves 1

nectarine, clementine and orange flower water juice

see variations page 92

The soothing flavour of orange flower water completes a fabulous fruity trio.

2 nectarines, halved and stoned
2 clementines, peeled
$^1/_2$ tsp orange flower water

Put the nectarines and clementines through a juice extractor. Pour into a glass, mix in the orange flower water and serve immediately.

Serves 1

papaya, strawberry and pistachio smoothie

see variations page 93

The addition of pistachio nuts brings a taste of the East to these summer fruits.

1 small papaya, peeled and deseeded
150 g (5½ oz) strawberries, hulled
25 g (1 oz) shelled unsalted pistachios
120 ml (4 fl oz) plain low-fat yoghurt
60 ml (2 fl oz) milk

Place all the ingredients into a blender and blend until smooth. Pour into a glass and serve immediately.

Serves 1

orange, date and orange flower water smoothie

see variations page 94

Oranges and dates are combined in many traditional Moroccan recipes. Here is a smoothie with the same North African flavours.

Zest and juice of 2 oranges
5 dried dates, stoned
240 ml (8 fl oz) plain low-fat yoghurt
½ tsp orange flower water

Place all the ingredients into a blender and blend until smooth. Pour into a glass and serve immediately.

Serves 1

green tea, apple and grape juice

see variations page 95

Not only is green tea reputed to have considerable health benefits; it also blends perfectly with fresh fruit to make unusual juices.

1 pinch maccha (green tea) powder
120 ml (4 fl oz) boiling water
1 apple
150 g (5$^{1}/_{2}$ oz) seedless green grapes

Mix the maccha powder with the boiling water and leave in the fridge to cool. Put the apple and grapes through a juice extractor. Mix the juice with the green tea and serve.

Serves 1

grapefruit, basil and strawberry crush

see variations page 96

Three fresh foods with very different flavours – acidic, herbal and sweet – meld surprisingly well because of their shared aromatic quality.

2 grapefruit, peeled
50 g (1¼ oz) strawberries, hulled
6 fresh basil leaves

Put the grapefruit and strawberries through a juice extractor. Pour into a blender with the basil and blend for 30 seconds. Pour into a glass and serve immediately.

Serves 1

watermelon and strawberry juice

see variations page 97

Try this juice in the summer when both fruits are at their peak of ripeness and sweetness.

450 g (1 lb) peeled and chopped watermelon
175 g (6 oz) strawberries, hulled

Put the watermelon and strawberries through a juice extractor. Pour into a glass and serve immediately.

Serves 1

variations

mandarin, lemongrass, chilli and mint juice

see base recipe page 71

mandarin, lime, lemongrass, chilli and mint juice
Prepare the basic recipe, adding the juice of ½ lime.

orange, lemongrass, chilli and mint juice
Prepare the basic recipe, omitting the mandarin oranges and replacing them with 3 peeled oranges.

mango, lemongrass, chilli and mint juice
Prepare the basic recipe, omitting the mandarin oranges and replacing them with 450 g (1 lb) peeled and chunked mango.

grapefruit, lemongrass, chilli and mint juice
Prepare the basic recipe, omitting the mandarin oranges and replacing them with ½ peeled grapefruit.

lychee, raspberry and rose water fizz

see base recipe page 72

lychee, strawberry and rose water fizz
Prepare the basic recipe, omitting the raspberries and replacing them with the same quantity of strawberries.

lychee, blueberry and rose water fizz
Prepare the basic recipe, omitting the raspberries and replacing them with the same quantity of blueberries.

lychee, redcurrant and rose water fizz
Prepare the basic recipe, omitting the raspberries and replacing them with the same quantity of redcurrants.

lychee, blackberry and rose water fizz
Prepare the basic recipe, omitting the raspberries and replacing them with the same quantity of blackberries.

variations

mango, coconut and lime smoothie

see base recipe page 75

mango, coconut, chilli and lime smoothie
Prepare the basic recipe, adding ½ deseeded red chilli before blending.

mango, coconut, mint and lime smoothie
Prepare the basic recipe, adding 8 fresh mint leaves before blending.

mango, coconut, basil and lime smoothie
Prepare the basic recipe, adding 8 fresh basil leaves before blending.

mango, coconut, chilli, mint and lime smoothie
Prepare the basic recipe, adding ½ deseeded red chilli and 6 fresh mint leaves to the ingredients before blending.

mango, coconut, pineapple and lime smoothie
Prepare the basic recipe, omitting ½ the mango and replacing it with 115 g (4 oz) peeled pineapple chunks.

pineapple, lemongrass and cardamom crush

see base recipe page 76

pineapple, lemongrass and chilli crush
Prepare the basic recipe, omitting the cardamom and replacing it with
1 deseeded red chilli.

pineapple, lemongrass and mint crush
Prepare the basic recipe, omitting the cardamom and replacing it with
8 fresh mint leaves.

pineapple, lemongrass and ginger crush
Prepare the basic recipe, omitting the cardamom and replacing it with a
2½-cm (1-inch) piece of peeled root ginger.

pineapple, ginger and chilli crush
Prepare the basic recipe, omitting the cardamom and lemongrass, and
replacing them with a 2½-cm (1-inch) piece of peeled root ginger and
½ deseeded red chilli.

variations

nectarine, clementine and orange flower water juice

see base recipe page 79

peach, clementine and orange flower water juice
Prepare the basic recipe, omitting the nectarines and replacing them with 2 peaches.

mango, clementine and orange flower water juice
Prepare the basic recipe, omitting the nectarines and replacing them with 225 g (8 oz) peeled and chopped mango.

pineapple, clementine and orange flower water juice
Prepare the basic recipe, omitting the nectarines and replacing them with 225 g (8 oz) peeled and chopped pineapple.

papaya, clementine and orange flower water juice
Prepare the basic recipe, omitting the nectarines and replacing them with 225 g (8 oz) peeled and chopped papaya.

nectarine, clementine and rose water juice
Prepare the basic recipe, adding ½ teaspoon rose water to the juice extractor along with the other ingredients.

papaya, strawberry and pistachio smoothie

see base recipe page 80

papaya, strawberry and mint smoothie
Prepare the basic recipe, omitting the pistachios and replacing them with
6 fresh mint leaves.

papaya, strawberry and rose water smoothie
Prepare the basic recipe, omitting the pistachios and replacing them with a
dash of rose water.

papaya, raspberry, pistachio and mint smoothie
Prepare the basic recipe, omitting the strawberries and replacing them with
the same quantity of raspberries.

papaya, blackberry, pistachio and mint smoothie
Prepare the basic recipe, omitting the strawberries and replacing them with
the same quantity of blackberries.

orange, date and orange flower water smoothie

see base recipe page 82

orange, raisin and orange flower water smoothie
Prepare the basic recipe, omitting the dates and replacing them with 35 g (1¼ oz) raisins.

orange, apricot and orange flower water smoothie
Prepare the basic recipe, omitting the dates and replacing them with 5 dried apricots.

orange and apricot smoothie
Prepare the basic recipe, omitting the dates and replacing them with the same quantity of dried apricots. Also omit the orange flower water.

orange and date smoothie
Prepare the basic recipe, omitting the orange flower water.

green tea, apple and grape juice

see base recipe page 83

green tea and apple juice
Prepare the basic recipe, omitting the grapes and increasing the quantity of apples to 2 apples.

green tea and peach juice
Prepare the basic recipe, omitting the grapes and apples, and replacing them with 3 stoned peaches.

green tea and mango juice
Prepare the basic recipe, omitting the grapes and apples, and replacing them with 225 g (8 oz) peeled and chopped mango.

green tea and pineapple juice
Prepare the basic recipe, omitting the grapes and apples, and replacing them with 225 g (8 oz) peeled and chopped pineapple.

variations

grapefruit, basil and strawberry crush

see base recipe page 84

orange, basil and strawberry crush
Prepare the basic recipe, omitting the grapefruit and replacing them with 3 peeled oranges.

mandarin, basil and strawberry crush
Prepare the basic recipe, omitting the grapefruit and replacing them with 5 peeled mandarin oranges.

apple, basil and strawberry crush
Prepare the basic recipe, omitting the grapefruit and replacing them with 3 apples.

pineapple, basil and strawberry crush
Prepare the basic recipe, omitting the grapefruit and replacing them with 330 g (11¼ oz) peeled and chopped pineapple.

watermelon and strawberry juice

see base recipe page 87

watermelon, strawberry and mint juice
Prepare the basic recipe, adding 8 fresh mint leaves to the ingredients before passing them through the juice extractor.

watermelon, strawberry and basil juice
Prepare the basic recipe, adding 8 fresh basil leaves to the ingredients before passing them through the juice extractor.

watermelon, strawberry and chilli juice
Prepare the basic recipe, adding ½ deseeded red chilli to the ingredients before passing them through the juice extractor.

watermelon, strawberry and lemongrass juice
Prepare the basic recipe, adding 1 trimmed lemongrass stalk to the ingredients before passing them through the juice extractor.

health tonics

All juices and smoothies are rich in vitamins and minerals, but the fruit-packed ones chosen for this chapter will offer a particularly strong boost to your immune system.

maxi 'C'

see variations page 116

Here's the ultimate pick-me-up for when you feel a cold coming on. This juice is packed full of vitamin C in its strongest and purest form.

150 g (5^1/$_2$ oz) blackcurrants
150 g (5^1/$_2$ oz) redcurrants
2 kiwi fruit, peeled
2 oranges, peeled

Put the blackcurrants, redcurrants, kiwi fruit and oranges through a juice extractor. Pour into a glass and serve immediately.

Serves 1

the energiser super juice

see variations page 117

This vegetable juice combines sweet roots and gentle greens, providing a tasty vitamin overload.

1 cooked beetroot, peeled and trimmed
2 carrots, peeled and trimmed
100g (3½ oz) baby spinach
¼ cucumber

Put all the ingredients through a juice extractor. Pour into a glass and serve immediately.

Serves 1

hangover cure

see variations page 118

An excellent hydrating juice to get you back to peak performance to face the day ahead.

1 apple
1 carrot, peeled and trimmed
2 celery stalks, trimmed
2-cm (³/₄-inch) piece of peeled root ginger
225 g (8 oz) mixed dried berries and currants

Put all the ingredients through a juice extractor. Pour into a glass and serve immediately.

Serves 1

diabetic juice

see variations page 119

This juice, which has the comforting flavours of a fruit crumble, is particularly beneficial for diabetics, as cinnamon is believed to have a positive effect on the digestive system.

3 apples
2 pears
Pinch of ground cinnamon

Put the apples and pears through a juice extractor. Pour into a glass and sprinkle with a pinch of cinnamon. Serve immediately.

Serves 1

cleansing juice

see variations page 120

Try this juice to help detoxify your system when you are feeling slightly the worse for wear. Its light flavour means that you can help cleanse the body while enjoying a refreshing drink.

2 apples
115 g (4 oz) peeled honeydew melon chunks
1/4 cucumber
50 g (1³/₄ oz) watercress
15 g (¹/₄ oz) wheatgrass (optional)

Put all the ingredients through a juice extractor. Pour into a glass and serve immediately.

Serves 1

cold remedy

see variations page 121

Manuka honey has antibacterial properties which will help you recover from a cold.

2 lemons, peeled
2-cm (^{3}/$_4$-inch) piece of fresh root ginger, peeled
1 tbsp manuka honey
180 ml (6 fl oz) boiling water
Sprig fresh rosemary

Put the lemons and ginger through a juice extractor. Put into a large mug and mix with the manuka honey, boiling water and rosemary. Let it steep for 5 minutes and drink.

Serves 1

yummy mummy juice

see variations page 122

Here's an ideal juice for expectant mothers, as it's full of folic acid, which is essential to nurture both mother and baby.

4 small broccoli florets
3 apples
Juice of ½ lime

Put the broccoli and apples through a juice extractor. Pour into a glass. Stir in the lime juice and serve immediately.

Serves 1

power smoothie

see variations page 123

Spirulina is a true super food. Packed full of antioxidants and rammed with vitamins, it has real health benefits. As it is not to everyone's taste, I have added it to a delicious smoothie to make it more drinkable.

1 banana, peeled and quartered
75 g (2³/₄ oz) mixed berries, plus 2 to garnish
250 ml (8 fl oz) plain low-fat yoghurt, plus 1 tsp to garnish
60 ml (2 fl oz) orange juice
1 tbsp spirulina powder

Place all the ingredients into a blender and blend for 1 minute or until smooth. Pour into a glass and serve immediately. Swirl in an extra teaspoonful of yoghurt and place two extra berries in the glass to garnish.

Serves 1

digestion smoothie

see variations page 124

This fibre-rich smoothie will aid your digestion system, and aside from its health benefits, it tastes wonderful.

1 banana, peeled and quartered
5 prunes, stoned
60 ml (2 fl oz) orange juice
240 ml (8 fl oz) plain low-fat yoghurt

Place all the ingredients into a blender and blend for 1 minute or until smooth. Pour into a glass or mug and serve immediately.

Serves 1

fat-burner smoothie

see variations page 125

Strictly speaking, this smoothie doesn't burn fat. Guarana, however, is said to speed up our metabolism, so it will definitely set you on your way toward exercising.

35 g (1¼ oz) strawberries, hulled
35 g (1¼ oz) raspberries
35 g (1¼ oz) blueberries
35 g (1¼ oz) cranberries
60 ml (2 fl oz) apple juice
1 tsp guarana powder
1 tbsp aloe vera juice

Place all the ingredients into a blender and blend for 1 minute or until smooth. Pour into a glass and serve immediately.

Serves 1

variations

maxi 'C'

see base recipe page 99

super 'C'
Prepare the basic recipe, omitting the black- and redcurrants, and replacing them with 150 g (5½ oz) blackberries and 120 g (4¼ oz) strawberries.

tropical 'C'
Prepare the basic recipe, omitting the black- and redcurrants, and replacing them with 225 g (8 oz) chopped mango and 225 g (8 oz) chopped papaya.

health plus 'C'
Prepare the basic recipe, omitting the kiwi fruit and adding another orange.

kiwi fruit and orange juice
Prepare the basic recipe, omitting the black- and redcurrants, and increasing the quantity of kiwi fruit to 4 and the oranges to 3.

variations

the energiser super juice

see base recipe page 100

5-a-day juice
Prepare the basic recipe, adding 1 deseeded red pepper before passing the ingredients through the juice extractor.

spinach and cucumber juice
Prepare the basic recipe, omitting the beetroot and carrots, and increasing the quantity of cucumber to 1 whole cucumber.

spicy super juice
Prepare the basic recipe, mixing in ½ tablespoon Worcestershire sauce and a dash of Tabasco sauce before serving.

beetroot, spinach and cucumber juice
Prepare the basic recipe, omitting the carrots and increasing the quantity of the beetroot to 3 small beetroots.

variations

hangover cure

see base recipe page 101

mixed berry, lemon and ginger juice
Prepare the basic recipe, omitting the apple, carrot and celery, and increasing the quantity of mixed berries and currants to 375 g (13 oz). Add ½ peeled lemon before putting the ingredients through the juice extractor.

mixed berry, apple and ginger juice
Prepare the basic recipe, omitting the carrot and celery, and increasing the quantity of mixed berries and currants to 300 g (10½ oz).

mixed berry and apple juice
Prepare the basic recipe, omitting the carrot, celery and ginger, and increasing the quantity of mixed berries and currants to 300 g (10½ oz) and the apples to 2.

mixed berry, orange and ginger juice
Prepare the basic recipe, omitting the carrot and celery, and increasing the quantity of mixed berries and currants to 300 g (10½ oz). Add 2 peeled oranges before putting the ingredients through the juice extractor.

variations

diabetic juice

see base recipe page 103

apple crumble juice
Prepare the basic recipe, omitting the pears and adding 2 more apples.

pear crumble juice
Prepare the basic recipe, omitting the apples and adding 3 more pears.

vanilla apple juice
Prepare the basic recipe, omitting the pears and adding 2 apples. When the juice is in a glass, sprinkle in the seeds from ¼ vanilla pod and add a squeeze of lemon juice. Stir to mix.

vanilla pear juice
Prepare the basic recipe, omitting the apples and adding 3 pears. When the juice is in a glass, sprinkle in the seeds from ¼ vanilla pod and add a squeeze of lemon juice. Stir to mix.

variations

cleansing juice

see base recipe page 104

cucumber and watercress juice
Prepare the basic recipe, omitting the apples and melon, and adding an extra ½ cucumber.

apple and melon juice
Prepare the basic recipe, omitting the cucumber and watercress. Replace them with another apple and an extra 115 g (4 oz) melon chunks.

apple and cucumber juice
Prepare the basic recipe, omitting the watercress and melon, and adding an extra ½ cucumber.

cucumber and mint juice
Prepare the basic recipe, omitting the apples, watercress and melon. Increase the quantity of cucumber to 1 whole cucumber and add a few leaves of fresh mint.

variations

cold remedy

see base recipe page 107

orange cold remedy
Prepare the basic recipe, omitting the lemons and replacing them with
1 large peeled orange.

orange and lemon cold remedy
Prepare the basic recipe, omitting 1 lemon and adding 1 orange.

grapefruit cold remedy
Prepare the basic recipe, omitting the lemons and replacing them with
1 peeled grapefruit.

extra-strength cold remedy
Prepare the basic recipe, adding 1 tablespoon French brandy to the mixture
before leaving it to steep.

yummy mummy juice

see base recipe page 108

broccoli, celery and apple juice
Prepare the basic recipe, omitting 1 broccoli floret and adding 1 celery stalk.

broccoli and lime juice
Prepare the basic recipe, omitting the apples and adding another
6 broccoli florets.

variations

power smoothie

see base recipe page 111

power smoothie with mixed greens
Prepare the basic recipe, omitting the spirulina and replacing it with
1 tablespoon mixed greens powder.

power smoothie with guarana
Prepare the basic recipe, omitting the spirulina and replacing it with
1 teaspoon guarana.

power smoothie with aloe vera
Prepare the basic recipe, omitting the spirulina and replacing it with
1 tablespoon aloe vera juice.

power smoothie with manuka honey
Prepare the basic recipe, omitting the spirulina and replacing it with
2 teaspoons manuka honey.

variations

digestion smoothie

see base recipe page 112

digestion smoothie with figs
Prepare the basic recipe, omitting the prunes and replacing them with
5 dried figs.

digestion smoothie with flax oil
Prepare the basic recipe, adding 1 tablespoon pure flax oil to the other
ingredients.

digestion smoothie with figs and flax oil
Prepare the basic recipe, omitting the prunes and replacing them with
5 dried figs. Add 1 tablespoon flax oil to the other ingredients.

super digestion smoothie
Prepare the basic recipe, adding 1 tablespoon pure flax oil and 2 dried figs to
the other ingredients.

variations

fat-burner smoothie

see base recipe page 115

fat burner with green tea
Prepare the basic recipe, omitting the apple juice and replacing it with
60 ml (2 fl oz) diluted green tea.

berry apple smoothie
Prepare the basic recipe, omitting the aloe vera juice and the guarana.

dairy fat burner
Prepare the basic recipe, omitting the apple juice and replacing it with
60 ml (2 fl oz) plain low-fat yoghurt.

fat burner with ginger
Prepare the basic recipe, adding 1 teaspoon peeled and grated root ginger to
the ingredients before blending.

juice boosts

Drinking a glass of pure juice, without any
thickening agent or artificial flavourings or
preservatives, is always an uplifting experience.
The sweetness and ripeness of the individual
ingredients comes through with a delicious clarity.
Try a few of these recipes and you'll soon be hooked
on juice-making.

green goddess

see variations page 144

A strange combination at first glance, but don't be fooled. This is a delicious and cleansing mix of fruit and vegetables, and great for the digestion.

2 celery stalks, trimmed and halved
1 apple
1 kiwi fruit, peeled
1 pear
Handful of baby spinach, washed
$1/2$ cucumber
Squeeze of lime juice

Put the celery, apple, kiwi fruit, pear, spinach and cucumber through a juice extractor. Pour into a glass. Top off with a squeeze of lime juice and serve immediately.

Serves 1

rise and shine

see variations page 145

A wonderful juice with the warm kick of ginger to liven up your breakfast smoothie.

2 apples
3 carrots, trimmed
2-cm (³/₄-inch) piece of fresh root ginger, peeled

Put all the ingredients through a juice extractor. Pour into a glass and serve immediately.

Serves 1

root juice

see variations page 146

The juice's vibrant intensity of colour means that it will always impress – and so will its sweet, nutty flavour.

2 large beetroots, trimmed
3 carrots, trimmed
2-cm ($^3/_4$-inch) piece fresh root ginger, peeled

Put all the ingredients through a juice extractor. Pour into a glass and serve immediately.

Serves 1

pure juice

see variations page 147

This thirst-quencher is light, refreshing and easy to drink. An Ogen melon would be a delicious choice, but any green-fleshed melon will do.

$^1/_3$ cucumber
225 g (8 oz) honeydew or Ogen melon,
    peeled and diced
1 celery stalk, trimmed
6 fresh mint leaves

Put all the ingredients through a juice extractor. Pour into a glass and serve immediately.

Serves 1

melon medley

see variations page 148

These three sweet melons make a magical combination that is perfect for children and adults alike.

1 large slice of watermelon, peeled and diced
1 large slice of cantaloupe melon, peeled and diced
1 large slice of honeydew or Ogen melon, peeled and diced

Put all the ingredients through a juice extractor. Pour into a glass and serve immediately.

Serves 1

orange, mango and lime juice

see variations page 149

If you've never tried freshly squeezed mango juice, you're in for a real treat with this juice. It's one of my favourites.

3 oranges, peeled
1 large mango, peeled, stoned and cut into chunks
Juice of $\frac{1}{2}$ lime

Put the oranges and mango through a juice extractor. Pour into a glass and top with the lime juice. Serve immediately.

Serves 1

cranberry, apple and orange juice

see variations page 150

The tart flavour of cranberries is very refreshing, and it makes this juice a real thirst-quencher.

115 g (4 oz) cranberries
2 apples
2 oranges, peeled

Put all the ingredients through a juice extractor. Pour into a glass and serve immediately.

Serves 1

carrot, apple, celery and beetroot juice

see variations page 151

For those who are a little frightened of beetroot juice, this is the perfect drink to get you acquainted. It is sweet, light and easy to drink.

1 carrot, trimmed
1 apple
1 celery stalk, trimmed
2 small beetroots, trimmed

Put all the ingredients through a juice extractor. Pour into a glass and serve immediately.

Serves 1

autumnal juice

see variations page 152

The mellow flavours of this juice, as well as the fact that the fruits are all harvested in the autumn, make it particularly suitable for drinking at that time.

2 apples
2 pears
150 g (5½ oz) blackberries

Put all the ingredients through a juice extractor. Pour into a glass and serve immediately.

Serves 1

vegetable juice

see variations page 153

This is a meal in a glass: full of flavour, vitamin C and essential minerals such as iron.

1 broccoli floret
2 celery stalks, trimmed
1 carrot, trimmed
1 red pepper, cored and deseeded
4 tomatoes
Small handful of parsley leaves
25 g (1 oz) watercress
Pinch of salt

Put all the ingredients through a juice extractor. Pour into a glass and serve immediately.

Serves 1

variations

green goddess

see base recipe page 127

apple and kiwi fruit green goddess
Prepare the basic recipe, omitting the pear, spinach and cucumber.
Replace them with 1 additional apple and 1 extra kiwi fruit.

apple and pear green goddess
Prepare the basic recipe, omitting the celery, spinach and cucumber.
Replace them with 1 additional apple and 1 extra pear.

cucumber, apple and celery juice
Prepare the basic recipe, omitting the pear, spinach and kiwi fruit.
Replace them with 1 additional apple and an extra ½ cucumber.

spinach, cucumber and celery juice
Prepare the basic recipe, omitting the apple, pear and kiwi fruit.
Increase the spinach to 2 handfuls, the cucumber to 1 whole cucumber
and the celery to 3 stalks.

variations

rise and shine

see base recipe page 128

carrot and apple juice
Prepare the basic recipe, omitting the ginger.

carrot and orange juice
Prepare the basic recipe, omitting the ginger and apples, and replacing
them with 2 peeled oranges.

carrot, orange and coriander juice
Prepare the basic recipe, omitting the apples and replacing them with
2 peeled oranges and a small handful of coriander leaves.

carrot, apple and mint juice
Prepare the basic recipe, omitting the ginger and replacing it with
6 mint leaves.

variations

root juice

see base recipe page 131

carrot and ginger juice
Prepare the basic recipe, omitting the beetroots and increasing the quantity
of carrots to 5.

beetroot, orange and ginger juice
Prepare the basic recipe, omitting the carrots and replacing them with
3 peeled oranges.

beetroot and carrot juice
Prepare the basic recipe, omitting the ginger.

beetroot and ginger juice
Prepare the basic recipe, omitting the carrots and adding another large
beetroot.

variations

pure juice

see base recipe page 132

melon and cucumber juice
Prepare the basic recipe, omitting the mint and celery, and increasing the
quantity of cucumber to ½ cucumber.

melon, cucumber and mint juice
Prepare the basic recipe, omitting the celery and increasing the quantity of
cucumber to ½ cucumber.

cucumber, apple and mint juice
Prepare the basic recipe, omitting the melon and celery, increasing the
quanrtity of cucumber to ½ cucumber and adding 2 whole apples.

cucumber and celery juice
Prepare the basic recipe, omitting the melon and mint, and increasing the
quantity of celery to 2 stalks and the cucumber to ½ cucumber.

melon medley

see base recipe page 133

melon and rose water juice
Prepare the basic recipe, mixing in 1 teaspoon rose water after pouring the juice into a glass.

melon and orange flower water juice
Prepare the basic recipe, mixing in 1 teaspoon orange flower water after pouring the juice into a glass.

melon and mint medley
Prepare the basic recipe, adding 6 mint leaves before putting the ingredients through a juice extractor.

melon and strawberry juice
Prepare the basic recipe, adding 6 large hulled strawberries before putting the ingredients through a juice extractor.

orange, mango and lime juice

see base recipe page 135

mango and lime juice
Prepare the basic recipe, omitting the oranges and adding another mango.

mango and passion fruit juice
Prepare the basic recipe, omitting the oranges and adding another mango.
Add the juice of 2 passion fruit along with the lime juice.

mango and pineapple juice
Prepare the basic recipe, omitting the oranges and adding 225 g (8 oz)
pineapple chunks.

mango, pineapple and passion fruit juice
Prepare the basic recipe, omitting the oranges and adding 225 g (8 oz)
pineapple chunks. Add the juice of 2 passion fruit along with the lime juice.

cranberry, apple and orange juice

see base recipe page 136

cranberry and apple juice
Prepare the basic recipe, omitting the oranges and replacing them with
2 more apples.

cranberry, orange and peach juice
Prepare the basic recipe, omitting the apples and replacing them with
1 peeled and stoned peach.

apple, orange and raspberry juice
Prepare the basic recipe, omitting 35 g (1¼ oz) fresh cranberries and
replacing them with 35 g (1¼ oz) raspberries.

cranberry, apple, orange and strawberry juice
Prepare the basic recipe, omitting 35 g (1¼ oz) fresh cranberries and
replacing them with 35 g (1¼ oz) hulled strawberries.

cranberry, apple, orange and mint juice
Prepare the basic recipe, adding 8 fresh mint leaves to the other ingredients.

variations

carrot, apple, celery and beetroot juice

see base recipe page 139

carrot, beetroot and celery juice
Prepare the basic recipe, omitting the apple and adding an extra carrot.

carrot, apple and beetroot juice
Prepare the basic recipe, omitting the celery and adding an extra apple.

beetroot and celery juice
Prepare the basic recipe, omitting the carrot and apple. Replace them with
an extra beetroot and 1 more celery stalk.

carrot, celery, beetroot and pear juice
Prepare the basic recipe, omitting the apple. Replace it with 1 peeled
and cored pear.

variations

autumnal juice

see base recipe page 140

apple, pear and raspberry juice
Prepare the basic recipe, omitting the blackberries and replacing them with 150 g (5½ oz) raspberries.

apple, pear and strawberry juice
Prepare the basic recipe, omitting the blackberries and replacing them with 150 g (5½ oz) hulled strawberries.

apple, pear and blueberry juice
Prepare the basic recipe, omitting the blackberries and replacing them with 150 g (5½ oz) blueberries.

apple, pear and orange juice
Prepare the basic recipe, omitting the blackberries and replacing them with 1 peeled orange.

variations

vegetable juice

see base recipe page 143

vegetable juice 'bloody mary'
Prepare the basic recipe. After putting the ingredients through a juice extractor, mix in 2 tablespoons vodka, ½ tablespoon Worcestershire sauce, a couple of dashes of Tabasco, a sprinkling of celery salt, a squeeze of lemon juice and a generous grinding of black pepper.

vegetable juice 'virgin mary'
Prepare the basic recipe. After putting the ingredients through a juice extractor, mix in ½ tablespoon Worcestershire sauce, a couple of dashes of Tabasco, a sprinkling of celery salt, a squeeze of lemon juice and a good grinding of black pepper.

vegetable juice with a spicy kick
Prepare the basic recipe, adding 1 teaspoon chilli sauce and a generous grinding of black pepper to the juice before serving.

vegetable juice with a zingy kick
Prepare the basic recipe, adding 1 teaspoon lemon juice and 1 teaspoon lime juice to the vegetable juice before serving.

blends for children

It can sometimes be hard to get children to

appreciate nutritious fruits and vegetables, but the

recipes in this chapter are all so delicious that they'll

be clamouring for more! Simply double, triple or

quadruple the ingredients to make enough to satisfy

the whole family.

apple, blackcurrant and elderflower juice

see variations page 172

A charmingly old-fashioned favourite that appeals as much to children today as it always has done.

2 apples
75 g (2³/₄ oz) blackcurrants
¹/₂ tbsp elderflower cordial

Put the apples and blackcurrants through a juice extractor. Pour into a glass and mix in the elderflower cordial. Serve immediately.

Serves 1

st. clement's juice

see variations page 173

'Oranges and lemons, say the bells of St. Clement's', goes the old nursery rhyme. Here's a simple, classic combination with a citrussy tang.

1 orange, peeled
3 clementines, peeled
1 lemon, peeled

Put all the ingredients through a juice extractor. Pour into a glass and serve immediately. You can also use a citrus squeezer for this recipe.

Serves 1

peach melba smoothie

see variations page 174

The classic Peach Melba, reconstructed: a simple peach smoothie with a raspberry coulis rippled through, giving each sweet mouthful a sour edge.

for the coulis

75 g (2³/₄ oz) raspberries
Squeeze of lemon juice
1 tsp honey

for the smoothie

2 peaches, peeled, stoned and quartered
120 ml (4 fl oz) plain low-fat yoghurt
60 ml (2 fl oz) milk

Place the coulis ingredients in the blender and blend until smooth. Pour out and set aside. If you do not want any seeds, pour the coulis through a mesh strainer. Don't worry about washing the blender, as it will give the peach smoothie a lovely pink colour.

Place the smoothie ingredients into the blender and blend the mixture for 1 minute or until smooth. Pour into a large bowl, swirl in the raspberry coulis then pour into a glass to serve.

Serves 1

peanut butter and jam smoothie

see variations page 175

This all-American sandwich favourite transfers beautifully to a sweet smoothie that children will love as a special lunch treat.

1 banana, peeled and quartered
1 tbsp strawberry jam
1 tbsp smooth peanut butter
120 ml (4 fl oz) plain low-fat yoghurt
60 ml (2 fl oz) milk

Put all the ingredients into a blender and blend until smooth. Pour into a glass and serve immediately.

Serves 1

chocolate marshmallow cloud shake

see variations page 176

A velvety rich chocolate shake dappled with soft bubbles of marshmallow – a comforting treat for children.

300 ml (10 fl oz) chocolate ice cream
2 tbsp milk
1 tbsp chocolate sauce
50 g (1³/₄ oz) miniature marshmallows

Place the chocolate ice cream and milk into a blender and blend until smooth. Pour into a bowl and swirl in the chocolate sauce and marshmallows. Pour into a glass and serve immediately.

Serves 1

banana and toffee smoothie

see variations page 177

This irresistibly rich smoothie is made sweet by the dulce de leche and satiny smooth by the yoghurt.

1½ bananas, peeled and quartered
1 tbsp dulce de leche
120 ml (4 fl oz) plain low-fat yoghurt
60 ml (2 fl oz) milk
1 ginger biscuit

Place the banana, dulce de leche, yoghurt and milk into a blender. Blend for 1 minute or until smooth. Pour into a glass and crumble the biscuit on top.

Serves 1

pineappleade

see variations page 178

A tangy twist on old-fashioned lemonade, this is perfect for pouring out of a tall pitcher on a long summer afternoon.

¼ pineapple, peeled
60 ml (2 fl oz) sparkling water

Put the pineapple through a juice extractor. Pour into a glass and top off with sparkling water.

Serves 1

strawberry and nectarine fizz

see variations page 179

Adding sparkling water to fresh juice makes a small amount of fruit go further. This recipe is also good in place of champagne for those who don't want to drink alcohol but have something to celebrate.

150 g (5¹/₂ oz) strawberries, hulled
2 nectarines, halved and stoned
60 ml (2 fl oz) sparkling water

Put the fruit through a juice extractor. Pour into a glass and top with the sparkling water.

Serves 1

strawberry cheesecake smoothie

see variations page 180

This smoothie looks like a cheesecake in reverse, with the crunchy cookie on top and creamy fruit 'filling' underneath.

150 g (5¹/₂ oz) strawberries, hulled
1 tbsp strawberry jam
120 ml (4 fl oz) mascarpone
120 ml (4 fl oz) plain low-fat yoghurt
1 tsp vanilla extract
1 ginger biscuit

Put the strawberries, jam, mascarpone, yoghurt and vanilla extract in a blender. Blend for 1 minute or until smooth. Pour into a glass and crumble the ginger biscuit on top.

Serves 1

monster juice

see variations page 181

The spooky green makes this juice perfect for Halloween – but kids will love it whatever the time of year.

1 kiwi fruit, peeled
150 g (5^1/$_2$ oz) seedless green grapes
225 g (8 oz) honeydew melon, peeled and chopped
3 green apples

Put all the ingredients through a juice extractor. Pour into a glass and serve immediately.

Serves 1

apple, blackcurrant and elderflower juice

see base recipe page 155

apple and elderflower juice
Prepare the basic recipe, omitting the blackcurrants and replacing them with 1 extra apple.

apple, blackberry and elderflower juice
Prepare the basic recipe, omitting the blackcurrants and replacing them with the same quantity of blackberries.

apple, raspberry and elderflower juice
Prepare the basic recipe, omitting the blackcurrants and replacing them with the same quantity of raspberries.

apple, strawberry and elderflower juice
Prepare the basic recipe, omitting the blackcurrants and replacing them with the same quantity of strawberries.

st. clement's juice

see base recipe page 156

orange and clementine juice
Prepare the basic recipe, omitting the lemon and replacing it with 1 extra peeled orange.

clementine, lemon and lime juice
Prepare the basic recipe, omitting the orange and replacing it with 1 peeled lime and ½ teaspoon sugar.

orange and lemon juice
Prepare the basic recipe, omitting the clementines and replacing them with 2 extra peeled oranges.

mandarin and lemon juice
Prepare the basic recipe, omitting the orange and clementines, and replacing them with 3 peeled mandarin oranges and ½ teaspoon sugar.

variations

peach melba smoothie

see base recipe page 159

strawberry and raspberry swirl smoothie
Prepare the basic smoothie recipe, omitting the peaches and replacing them with the same quantity of strawberries.

peach and blueberry swirl smoothie
Prepare the basic coulis recipe, omitting the raspberries and replacing them with the same quantity of blueberries.

mango and raspberry swirl smoothie
Prepare the basic smoothie recipe, omitting the peaches and replacing them with 225 g (8 oz) chopped mango.

banana and raspberry swirl smoothie
Prepare the basic smoothie recipe, omitting the peaches and replacing them with 1½ bananas.

variations

peanut butter and jam smoothie

see base recipe page 160

peanut butter and raspberry jam smoothie
Prepare the basic recipe, omitting the strawberry jam and replacing it with
the same quantity of raspberry jam.

peanut butter and blackberry jam smoothie
Prepare the basic recipe, omitting the strawberry jam and replacing it with
the same quantity of blackberry jam.

peanut butter and blackcurrant jam smoothie
Prepare the basic recipe, omitting the strawberry jam and replacing it with
the same quantity of blackcurrant jam.

peanut butter and marmalade smoothie
Prepare the basic recipe, omitting the strawberry jam and replacing it with
the same quantity of orange marmalade.

peanut butter and chocolate smoothie
Prepare the basic recipe, omitting the strawberry jam and replacing it with
the same quantity of chocolate spread.

variations

chocolate marshmallow cloud shake

see base recipe page 163

white chocolate marshmallow cloud shake
Prepare the basic recipe, omitting the chocolate ice cream and replacing it with the same quantity of white chocolate ice cream.

white chocolate and strawberry swirl shake
Prepare the basic recipe, omitting the chocolate ice cream and replacing it with the same quantity of white chocolate ice cream. Replace the chocolate sauce with strawberry sauce.

chocolate swirl shake
Prepare the basic recipe, omitting the marshmallows.

chocolate orange marshmallow cloud milkshake
Prepare the basic recipe, omitting the chocolate sauce and replacing it with the same quantity of rind-free marmalade, thinned down with 1 tablespoon warm water.

mocha marshmallow cloud milkshake
Prepare the basic recipe, adding 1 shot (2 tablespoons) espresso.

variations

banana and toffee smoothie

see base recipe page 164

banana, toffee and chocolate smoothie
Prepare the basic recipe, topping the glass with a shower of finely grated chocolate.

banana and chocolate smoothie
Prepare the basic recipe, omitting the dulce de leche and replacing it with the same amount of chocolate sauce.

strawberry and toffee smoothie
Prepare the basic recipe, omitting the bananas and adding 150 g (5½ oz) hulled strawberries.

peach and toffee smoothie
Prepare the basic recipe, omitting the bananas and adding 2 stoned and quartered peaches.

variations

pineappleade

see base recipe page 166

pineappleade with mint
Prepare the basic recipe, pouring the pineappleade into an iced glass and topping with fresh mint leaves.

orangeade
Prepare the basic recipe, omitting the pineapple and replacing it with 3 peeled oranges.

appleade
Prepare the basic recipe, omitting the pineapple and replacing it with 3 apples.

lemonade
Prepare the basic recipe, omitting the pineapple and replacing it with 3 peeled lemons. Mix in 1 tablespoon sugar after putting the lemons through the juice extractor.

cherryade
Prepare the basic recipe, omitting the strawberries and replacing them with 150 g (5½ oz) stoned cherries.

strawberry and nectarine fizz

see base recipe page 167

strawberry fizz
Prepare the basic recipe, omitting the nectarines and increasing the quantity of strawberries to 300 g (10½ oz).

raspberry and nectarine fizz
Prepare the basic recipe, omitting the strawberries and replacing them with the same quantity of raspberries.

nectarine fizz
Prepare the basic recipe, omitting the strawberries and replacing them with an additional ½ nectarine.

strawberry and raspberry fizz
Prepare the basic recipe, omitting the nectarine and replacing it with 150 g (5½ oz) raspberries.

variations

strawberry cheesecake smoothie

see base recipe page 168

blackberry cheesecake smoothie
Prepare the basic recipe, omitting the strawberries and jam, and replacing them with the same quantities of blackberries and blackberry jam.

raspberry cheesecake smoothie
Prepare the basic recipe, omitting the strawberries and jam, and replacing them with the same quantities of raspberries and raspberry jam.

rhubarb cheesecake smoothie
Prepare the basic recipe, omitting the strawberries and jam, and replacing them with the same quantities of stewed, sweetened rhubarb and rhubarb jam.

vanilla cheesecake smoothie
Prepare the basic recipe, omitting the strawberries and jam, and replacing them with an extra 60 ml (2 fl oz) mascarpone.

variations

monster juice

see base recipe page 171

monster juice with worms
Prepare the basic recipe, adding some jelly worms to the glass for an extra scare.

red monster juice
Make the monster juice using 1 purple plum, 150 g (5½ oz) seedless red grapes, 225 g (8 oz) chopped watermelon and 3 red apples instead of the fruits listed in the basic recipe.

grape and kiwi fruit juice
Prepare the basic recipe, omitting the green melon and apples. Add an extra kiwifruit and an extra 150 g (5½ oz) of grapes.

melon and grape juice
Prepare the basic recipe, omitting the kiwi fruit and apples, and increasing the quantity of grapes to 225 g (8 oz) and the melon to 340 g (11 oz).

milkshakes

Where the principal ingredient of a smoothie is fresh fruit, in a milkshake it is rich, thick ice cream. All the drinks in this chapter are delightfully smooth and frothy.

banana milkshake

see variations page 198

This milkshake, which we all grew up on, never loses its charm.

1 banana, peeled and quartered
300 ml (10 fl oz) vanilla ice cream
2 tbsp milk

Place all the ingredients into a blender and blend for 1 minute. Pour into a glass and serve immediately.

Serves 1

raspberry and white chocolate milkshake

see variations page 199

Choose the best-quality ice cream you can find, as it makes a real difference here.

115 g (4 oz) raspberries
300 ml (10 fl oz) white chocolate ice cream
2 tbsp milk

Place all the ingredients into a blender and blend for 1 minute. Pour into a glass and serve immediately.

Serves 1

mixed berry milkshake

see variations page 200

The flavours of mixed berries make a wonderfully cooling summer drink.

150 g (5¹/₂ oz) each of blueberries, blackberries, strawberries and raspberries
300 ml (10 fl oz) vanilla ice cream
2 tbsp milk

Place all the ingredients into a blender and blend for 1 minute. Pour into a glass and serve immediately.

Serves 1

pear, chocolate and ginger milkshake

see variations page 201

Pear with chocolate is an inspired combination that has consistently found favor. This smooth shake is sure to become one of your favourites.

2^1/$_2$-cm (1-inch) piece of fresh root ginger
1 ripe pear
300 ml (10 fl oz) chocolate ice cream
2 tbsp milk

Peel and grate the ginger. Peel and chop the pear. Place all the ingredients into a blender and blend for 1 minute. Pour into a glass and serve immediately.

Serves 1

chocolate and orange milkshake

see variations page 202

A delicious variation on the standard plain chocolate shake.

Juice of 1 small orange
Grated rind of ½ orange
300 ml (10 fl oz) chocolate ice cream
2 tbsp milk
3 tbsp cornstarch

Put all the ingredients into a blender and blend for 1 minute. Pour into a glass and serve immediately.

Serves 1

strawberry and mint lassi

see variations page 203

The lassi is a milk and yoghurt shake from India. It is every bit as cooling as you would expect.

8 strawberries, hulled
240 ml (8 fl oz) milk
120 ml (4 fl oz) plain low-fat yoghurt
1 tsp sugar
4 fresh mint leaves

Put all the ingredients into a blender and blend for 1 minute. Pour into a glass and serve immediately.

Serves 1

mango and cardamom lassi

see variations page 204

This lassi has an authentic Indian flavour as it pairs the favourite fruit of the subcontinent with a traditional Indian spice.

Seeds from 2 cardamom pods
1 mango, peeled, stoned and cut into chunks
240 ml (8 fl oz) milk
120 ml (4 fl oz) plain low-fat yoghurt
1 tsp sugar (optional)

Grind the cardamom seeds slightly with a mortar and pestle. Place all the ingredients into a blender and blend for 1 minute. Pour into a glass and serve immediately.

Serves 1

watermelon and strawberry milkshake

see variations page 205

Milkshakes are sometimes seen as the preserve of children, but this light and fragrant shake will be appreciated by adults too.

115 g (4 oz) peeled watermelon chunks
115 g (4 oz) strawberries, hulled
240 ml (8 fl oz) ice cream
2 tbsp milk

Place all the ingredients into a blender and blend until for 1 minute or until smooth. Pour into a glass and serve immediately.

Serves 1

variations

banana milkshake

see base recipe page 183

banana malt shake
Prepare the basic recipe, adding 1 tablespoon malt powder to the ingredients before blending.

banana and peanut butter malt shake
Prepare the basic recipe, adding 1 tablespoon malt powder and 1 tablespoon peanut butter to the ingredients before blending.

banana and chocolate milkshake
Prepare the basic recipe, omitting the vanilla ice cream and replacing it with the same quantity of chocolate ice cream.

banana and chocolate malt shake
Prepare the basic recipe, omitting the vanilla ice cream and replacing it with the same quantity of chocolate ice cream. Also add 1 tablespoon malt powder to the ingredients before blending.

raspberry and white chocolate milkshake

see base recipe page 184

raspberry and white chocolate malt shake
Prepare the basic recipe, adding 1 tablespoon malt powder to the other ingredients before blending.

white chocolate milkshake
Prepare the basic recipe, omitting the raspberries and increasing the quantity of ice cream to 360 ml (12 fl oz).

white chocolate malt shake
Prepare the basic recipe, omitting the raspberries and increasing the quantity of ice cream to 360 ml (12 fl oz). Add 1 tablespoon malt powder to the other ingredients before blending.

double chocolate milkshake
Prepare the basic recipe, omitting the raspberries and adding 120 ml (4 fl oz) white chocolate ice cream and 1 tablespoon chocolate chips to the other ingredients before blending.

variations

mixed berry milkshake

see base recipe page 187

mixed berry malt shake
Prepare the basic recipe, adding 1 tablespoon malt powder to the other ingredients before blending.

mixed berry and rose water milkshake
Prepare the basic recipe, adding 1 tablespoon rose water to the other ingredients before blending.

mixed berry and chocolate milkshake
Prepare the basic recipe, omitting the vanilla ice cream and replacing it with the same quantity of chocolate ice cream.

mixed berry and ginger ice cream
Prepare the basic recipe, omitting the vanilla ice cream and replacing it with the same quantity of ginger ice cream.

variations

pear, chocolate and ginger milkshake

see base recipe page 188

indulgent pear, chocolate and ginger milkshake
Prepare the basic recipe, topping the milkshake with 1 crumbled ginger biscuit just before serving.

pear, chocolate and ginger malt shake
Prepare the basic recipe, adding 1 tablespoon malt powder to the other ingredients before blending.

pear and chocolate milkshake
Prepare the basic recipe, omitting the root ginger.

pear and double chocolate milkshake
Prepare the basic recipe, omitting the root ginger. Top the milkshake with 1 teaspoon chocolate sprinkles just before serving.

variations

chocolate and orange milkshake

see base recipe page 191

chocolate orange malt shake
Prepare the basic recipe, adding 1 tablespoon malt powder to the other ingredients before blending.

mint chocolate milkshake
Prepare the basic recipe, omitting the orange zest and juice, and replacing them with a few drops of mint extract. Increase the quantity of ice cream to 360 ml (12 fl oz).

chocolate and coffee milkshake
Prepare the basic recipe, omitting the orange juice and zest, and replacing them with 1 teaspoon good-quality instant coffee granules dissolved in 1 tablespoon boiling water.

chocolate and toffee milkshake
Prepare the basic recipe, omitting the orange juice and zest and replacing them with 1 tablespoon dulce de leche.

strawberry and mint lassi

see base recipe page 192

strawberry, mint and rose water lassi
Prepare the basic recipe, adding 1 teaspoon rose water to the other
ingredients before blending.

strawberry lassi
Prepare the basic recipe, omitting the mint.

strawberry and rose water lassi
Prepare the basic recipe, omitting the mint and adding 1 teaspoon rose
water to the other ingredients before blending.

strawberry, lychee and rose water lassi
Prepare the basic recipe, omitting the mint and adding 1 teaspoon
rose water and 4 peeled and stoned lychees to the other ingredients
before blending.

mango and cardamom lassi

see base recipe page 195

mango lassi
Prepare the basic recipe, omitting the cardamom.

mango and lemon grass lassi
Prepare the basic recipe, omitting the cardamom and replacing it with ½ lemon grass stalk, finely chopped.

mango and chilli lassi
Prepare the basic recipe, omitting the cardamom and replacing it with ½ deseeded red chilli.

mango and mint lassi
Prepare the basic recipe, omitting the cardamom and replacing it with 4 fresh mint leaves.

mango, cardamom and coconut milk lassi
Prepare the basic recipe, omitting the milk and replacing it with the same amount of coconut milk.

watermelon and strawberry milkshake

see base recipe page 196

watermelon and strawberry malt shake
Prepare the basic recipe, adding 1 tablespoon malt powder to the ingredients before blending.

watermelon, strawberry and rose water milkshake
Prepare the basic recipe, adding 1 teaspoon rose water to the ingredients before blending.

watermelon milkshake
Prepare the basic recipe, omitting the strawberries and increasing the quantity of watermelon to 225 g (8 oz).

watermelon and raspberry milkshake
Prepare the basic recipe, omitting the strawberries and replacing them with 150 g (5½ oz) raspberries.

honeydew and strawberry milkshake
Prepare the basic recipe, omitting the watermelon and replacing them with an equal quantity of honeydew melon.

thick and frosty

These thick shakes and smoothies are especially good when chilled and served ice-cold. Many of them contain crushed ice as a thickening and cooling ingredient – making them just right for a hot summer day.

mango, pineapple and papaya ice cream smoothie

see variations page 224

A wonderfully exotic liquid ice cream.

$^1/_2$ mango, peeled and stoned
115 g (4 oz) pineapple chunks
$^1/_2$ small papaya, peeled and deseeded
120 ml (4 fl oz) vanilla ice cream
4 ice cubes

Place all the ingredients into a blender and blend for 1 minute. Pour into a glass and serve immediately.

Serves 1

chocolate and pistachio smoothie

see variations page 225

Pistachios combine wonderfully with lots of ingredients, especially chocolate. Try this drink for a satisfying and delicious treat.

35 g (1¼ oz) shelled unsalted pistachios
300 ml (10 fl oz) chocolate ice cream
3 tbsp milk

Place all the ingredients into a blender and blend for 1 minute. Pour into a glass and serve immediately.

Serves 1

white chocolate and apricot smoothie

see variations page 226

You can use either fresh or soft dried apricots in this recipe. The soft dried fruit make for a slightly stronger flavour, but are equally delicious.

75 g (2¾ oz) soft dried apricots or
150 g (5½ oz) fresh stoned apricots
300 ml (10 fl oz) white chocolate ice cream
3 tbsp milk

Put all the ingredients into a blender and blend for 1 minute. Pour into a glass and serve immediately.

Serves 1

mint chocolate chip smoothie

see variations page 227

Mint-flavoured chocolates are a classic after-dinner treat. Here is a liquid version.

300 ml (10 fl oz) mint chocolate chip ice cream
3 tbsp milk
1 tbsp chocolate chips

Put all the ingredients into a blender. Blend for 1 minute. Pour into a glass and serve immediately.

Serves 1

mocha frosty

see variations page 228

Coffee and chocolate – always a popular combination – is especially good in this refreshing and sustaining thick shake.

1 tsp instant coffee granules dissolved in 1 tbsp boiling water
240 ml (8 fl oz) chocolate ice cream
3 tbsp milk

Place all the ingredients into a blender and blend for 1 minute. Pour into a glass and serve immediately.

Serves 1

banana, pineapple and coconut frosty

see variations page 229

This really refreshing drink will bring a taste of the Caribbean to your kitchen.

1 banana, peeled and quartered
75 g (2³/₄ oz) peeled pineapple chunks
240 ml (8 fl oz) coconut ice cream
120 ml (4 fl oz) coconut milk

Place all the ingredients into a blender and blend for 1 minute. Pour into a glass and serve immediately.

Serves 1

raspberry and pineapple granita

see variations page 230

This superbly fruity combination is even more refreshing when sipped through ice. It also makes an excellent non-alcoholic party drink.

150 g (5½ oz) raspberries
½ pineapple, peeled and cored
2 glassfuls ice cubes

Put the fruit through a juice extractor, and then transfer it to a blender with the ice cubes. Blend until everything is combined. Pour into a glass and serve immediately.

Serves 1

watermelon and mint granita

see variations page 231

A light and fragrant combination that both looks and tastes exotic, refreshing and even luxurious.

350 g (12 oz) peeled watermelon chunks
1 glassful ice cubes
3 sprigs fresh mint

Put the watermelon through a juice extractor. Transfer it into a blender over the ice cubes and leaves from the mint sprigs. Blend for 1 minute. Pour into a glass and serve immediately. Garnish the glass with an additional mint sprig if desired.

Serves 1

coffee granita

see variations page 232

This drink makes an ideal refreshment to be served after a summer meal.

1 tsp instant coffee dissolved in 1 tbsp boiling water
1 tsp sugar (optional)
$\frac{1}{2}$ glass ice cubes

Place all the ingredients into a blender and blend for 1 minute. Pour into a shot glass or espresso cup and serve immediately.

Serves 1

papaya and lime granita

see variations page 233

The bold tropical flavours and crushed ice make this drink a real refresher.

1 papaya, peeled and deseeded
2 glassfuls ice cubes
Juice of 1 lime

Put the papaya through a juicer. Pour over the ice cubes and lime juice in a blender, and blend for 1 minute. Pour into a glass and serve immediately.

Serves 1

variations

mango, pineapple and papaya ice cream smoothie

see base recipe page 207

mango and papaya ice cream smoothie
Prepare the basic recipe, omitting the pineapple and replacing it with another ½ mango.

mango, passion fruit and papaya ice cream smoothie
Prepare the basic recipe, omitting the pineapple and replacing it with another ½ mango and the juice of 2 passion fruit.

mango, pineapple, passion fruit and papaya ice cream smoothie
Prepare the basic recipe, adding the juice of 2 passion fruit to the ingredients before blending.

boozy mango and papaya ice cream smoothie
Prepare the basic recipe, omitting the pineapple and replacing it with another ½ mango and 2 tablespoons dark rum.

chocolate and pistachio smoothie

see base recipe page 208

chocolate and almond smoothie
Prepare the basic recipe, omitting the pistachios and replacing them with the same quantity of almonds.

chocolate, pistachio and orange flower water smoothie
Prepare the basic recipe, adding ½ teaspoon orange flower water to the ingredients before blending.

white chocolate and pistachio smoothie
Prepare the basic recipe, omitting the chocolate ice cream and replacing it with the same quantity of white chocolate ice cream.

white chocolate, pistachio and orange flower water smoothie
Prepare the basic recipe, omitting the chocolate ice cream and replacing it with the same quantity of white chocolate ice cream. Add ½ teaspoon orange flower water to the other ingredients before blending.

white chocolate and apricot smoothie

see base recipe page 210

white chocolate and vanilla smoothie
Prepare the basic recipe, omitting the apricots and replacing them with ½ teaspoon vanilla extract.

white chocolate and caramel smoothie
Prepare the basic recipe, omitting the apricots and replacing them with 1 tablespoon dulce de leche.

white chocolate and mint smoothie
Prepare the basic recipe, omitting the apricots and replacing them with ½ teaspoon mint extract.

white chocolate and strawberry smoothie
Prepare the basic recipe, omitting the apricots and replacing them with the same quantity of strawberries.

variations

mint chocolate chip smoothie

see base recipe page 211

double mint chocolate chip smoothie
Prepare the basic recipe, adding 2 tablespoons chocolate sauce to
the ingredients before blending.

rich mint chocolate chip smoothie
Prepare the basic recipe, omitting the milk and replacing it with
4 tablespoons double cream.

boozy mint chocolate chip smoothie
Prepare the basic recipe, adding 2 tablespoons crème de menthe to
the ingredients before blending.

mint cream chocolate chip smoothie
Prepare the basic recipe, adding 2 broken-up mint cream sweets
when blending the other ingredients.

variations

mocha frosty

see base recipe page 212

rich mocha frosty
Prepare the basic recipe, omitting the milk and replacing it with
4 tablespoons double cream.

double chocolate mocha frosty
Prepare the basic recipe, adding 1 tablespoon chocolate chips to the other
ingredients before blending.

triple chocolate mocha frosty
Prepare the basic recipe, adding 1 tablespoon chocolate chips and
1 tablespoon chocolate sauce to the other ingredients before blending.

white chocolate mocha frosty
Prepare the basic recipe, omitting the chocolate ice cream and replacing it
with the same quantity of white chocolate ice cream.

variations

banana, pineapple and coconut frosty

see base recipe page 215

boozy banana and coconut frosty
Prepare the basic recipe, adding 2 tablespoons dark rum to the other ingredients before blending.

malibu, banana, pineapple and coconut frosty
Prepare the basic recipe, adding 2 tablespoons Malibu coconut-flavoured rum to the other ingredients before blending.

banana and coconut frosty
Prepare the basic recipe, omitting the pineapple and replacing it with another ½ banana. Also add 1 tablespoon chocolate chips to the other ingredients before blending.

papaya, pineapple and coconut frosty
Prepare the basic recipe, omitting the banana and replacing it with 350 g (12 oz) peeled and chunked papaya.

variations

raspberry and pineapple granita

see base recipe page 216

raspberry granita
Prepare the basic recipe, omitting the pineapple and replacing it with an extra 300 g (10½ oz) raspberries.

pineapple granita
Prepare the basic recipe, omitting the raspberries and adding another ¼ pineapple.

pineapple and strawberry granita
Prepare the basic recipe, omitting the raspberries and replacing them with the same quantity of strawberries.

raspberry and apple granita
Prepare the basic recipe, omitting the pineapple and replacing it with 3 apples.

lemon and pineapple granita
Prepare the basic recipe, omitting the raspberries and replacing with 2 tablespoons fresh lemon juice and 1 tablespoon sugar syrup.

watermelon and mint granita

see base recipe page 219

strawberry and mint granita
Prepare the basic recipe, omitting the watermelon and replacing it with 350 g (12 oz) strawberries.

mango and mint granita
Prepare the basic recipe, omitting the watermelon and replacing it with 450 g (1 lb) peeled and chunked mango.

apple and mint granita
Prepare the basic recipe, omitting the watermelon and replacing it with 3 apples.

orange and mint granita
Prepare the basic recipe, omitting the watermelon and replacing it with 3 oranges.

variations

coffee granita

see base recipe page 220

creamy coffee granita
Prepare the basic recipe, adding 1 tablespoon double cream to the other ingredients before blending.

mocha granita
Prepare the basic recipe, adding 1 teaspoon cocoa powder to the other ingredients before blending.

coffee liqueur granita
Prepare the basic recipe, adding 1 tablespoon Tia Maria or Kahlúa liqueur to the other ingredients before blending.

flavored coffee granita
Prepare the basic recipe, adding 1 tablespoon flavoured syrup (hazelnut, vanilla or mint are all good here) to the other ingredients before blending.

baileys coffee granita
Prepare the basic recipe, adding 1 tablespoon Baileys to the other ingredients before blending.

papaya and lime granita

see base recipe page 223

papaya and grapefruit granita
Prepare the basic recipe, omitting the lime and replacing it with the juice of
1 grapefruit.

papaya and orange granita
Prepare the basic recipe, omitting the lime and replacing it with the juice of
1 orange.

papaya and lemon granita
Prepare the basic recipe, omitting the lime and replacing it with the juice of
1 lemon.

papaya and mandarin granita
Prepare the basic recipe, omitting the lime and replacing it with the juice of
2 mandarin oranges.

naughty but nice

These sweet treats are the perfect comfort food – smooth, cool, creamy drinks to brighten your day. Any of the recipes in this chapter would be perfect for a tasty dessert.

strawberries and cream smoothie

see variations page 248

Afternoon teas on the lawn in the lazy, hazy days of long-ago summers always included strawberries and cream. Here is a liquid version.

75 g (2¾ oz) strawberries, hulled
300 ml (10 fl oz) strawberry ice cream
2 tbsp double cream
1 whole strawberry (optional)

Put all the ingredients into a blender and blend for 1 minute. Pour into a glass, decorate with 1 whole strawberry and serve immediately.

Serves 1

black forest smoothie

see variations page 249

A basic chocolate cherry smoothie is enriched by the addition of meltingly soft pieces of chocolate sponge cake.

200g (7 oz) stoned black cherries
300 ml (10 fl oz) chocolate ice cream
2 tbsp double cream
115 g (3¹/₂ oz) chopped chocolate sponge cake

Put the black cherries, ice cream and double cream into a blender and blend for 1 minute. Pour into a glass and stir in the chocolate sponge cake. Serve immediately.

Serves 1

mango, mandarin and coconut smoothie

see variations page 250

A sweet and creamy drink that captures the flavours of South-east Asia.

1 mango, peeled and stoned
1 mandarin orange, peeled and seeds removed
300 ml (10 fl oz) coconut ice cream
120 ml (4 fl oz) coconut milk

Put all the ingredients into a blender and blend for 1 minute. Pour into a glass and serve immediately.

Serves 1

tiramisu smoothie

see variations page 251

The sensational Italian pudding converts easily into a luxurious drink that would make a stylish conclusion to a party meal.

240 ml (8 fl oz) vanilla ice cream
120 ml (4 fl oz) mascarpone
1 tbsp double cream
1 sponge finger
1 tsp instant coffee dissolved in 1 tbsp boiling water
Cocoa powder for dusting

Put the ice cream, mascarpone and cream in a blender. Blend for 1 minute. Pour into a glass. Roughly crumble the sponge finger into the dissolved coffee. Stir the mixture into the glass. Dust the top of the mixture with the cocoa powder. Serve immediately.

Serves 1

strawberry trifle smoothie

see variations page 252

This once-maligned British pudding has been revalued and reworked in many kitchens recently. It's especially delicious as a smoothie.

150 g (5½ oz) strawberries, hulled
240 ml (8 fl oz) vanilla ice cream
120 ml (4 fl oz) ready-made custard
1 sponge finger, crumbled
Sugar sprinkles to serve

Put the strawberries, ice cream and custard into a blender and blend for 1 minute. Pour into a glass and stir the crumbled sponge finger through the mixture. Serve with the sugar sprinkles scattered on top.

Serves 1

banana, cream and chocolate smoothie

see variations page 253

This was my favourite pudding as a child – and it's still tempting. Feel free to replace the grated milk chocolate with an equivalent amount of your favourite chocolate bar.

1 banana, peeled and quartered
300 ml (10 fl oz) vanilla ice cream
2 tbsp double cream
1 tbsp milk chocolate, grated

Put the banana, ice cream and cream into a blender and blend for 1 minute. Pour into a glass and sprinkle the grated chocolate over the top. Serve immediately.

Serves 1

ginger and pear pudding smoothie

see variations page 254

Ginger brings a spicy warmth to this fruity smoothie.

1 ripe pear, peeled, cored and quartered
300 ml (10 fl oz) ginger ice cream
3 tbsp double cream
2 ginger biscuits, crumbled

Put all the ingredients except the ginger biscuits into a blender and blend for 1 minute. Pour into a glass and top with the crumbled biscuits. Serve immediately.

Serves 1

apple crumble smoothie

see variations page 255

Apple crumble topped with vanilla ice cream is a very popular desssert, especially in the autumn. Here the crumble and ice cream are blended into one rich smoothie.

225 g (8 oz) stewed apples
¼ tsp cinnamon
240 ml (8 fl oz) vanilla ice cream
3 tbsp double cream
1 oatmeal biscuit, crumbled

Put all the ingredients except the crumbled cookie into a blender and blend for 1 minute. Pour into a glass and top with the crumbled biscuit. Serve immediately.

Serves 1

strawberries and cream smoothie

see base recipe page 235

pavlova smoothie
Prepare the basic recipe, stirring through 50 g (1¾ oz) crushed meringues before serving.

peaches and cream smoothie
Prepare the basic recipe, omitting the strawberries and strawberry ice cream, and replacing them with 1 stoned and peeled peach and 300 ml (10 fl oz) vanilla ice cream.

raspberries and cream smoothie
Prepare the basic recipe, omitting the strawberries and strawberry ice cream and replacing them with 75 g (2¾ oz) raspberries and 300 ml (10 fl oz) raspberry frozen yoghurt or vanilla ice cream.

berries and cream smoothie
Prepare the basic recipe, omitting the strawberries and replacing them with 75 g (5½ oz) mixed berries.

peach melba and cream smoothie
Prepare the basic recipe, omitting the strawberries and strawberry ice cream and replacing them with 1 peeled and stoned peach and 300 ml (10 fl oz) raspberry-flavoured frozen yoghurt.

variations

black forest smoothie

see base recipe page 236

boozy black forest smoothie
Prepare the basic recipe, adding 2 tablespoons kirsch to the other ingredients before blending.

chocolate and cherry milkshake
Prepare the basic recipe, omitting the chocolate cake.

chocolate and cherry malt shake
Prepare the basic recipe, omitting the chocolate cake and adding 1 tablespoon malt powder to the other ingredients before blending.

double chocolate black cherry smoothie
Prepare the basic recipe, omitting the chocolate cake and replacing it with 1 tablespoon chocolate chips.

variations

mango, mandarin and coconut smoothie

see base recipe page 239

mandarin, pineapple and coconut smoothie
Prepare the basic recipe, omitting the mango and replacing it with 450 g
(1 lb) peeled and chunked pineapple.

mango, pineapple and coconut smoothie
Prepare the basic recipe, omitting the mandarin orange and replacing it with
60 ml (2 fl oz) pineapple juice.

mango and coconut ice cream smoothie
Prepare the basic recipe, omitting the mandarin orange and replacing it with
60 ml (2 fl oz) mango juice.

coconut smoothie
Prepare the basic recipe, omitting the mango and mandarin orange, and
increasing the quantity of coconut milk to 240 ml (8 fl oz).

variations

tiramisu smoothie

see base recipe page 240

marsala wine tiramisu smoothie
Prepare the basic recipe, adding 2 tablespoons Marsala wine to the
diluted coffee.

amaretto tiramisu smoothie
Prepare the basic recipe, adding 2 tablespoons amaretto liqueur to the
diluted coffee.

coffee liqueur tiramisu smoothie
Prepare the basic recipe, adding 2 tablespoons coffee liqueur (such as
Kahlúa or Tia Maria) to the diluted coffee.

baileys tiramisu smoothie
Prepare the basic recipe, adding 2 tablespoons Baileys liqueur to the
diluted coffee.

variations

strawberry trifle smoothie

see base recipe page 242

raspberry trifle smoothie
Prepare the basic recipe, omitting the strawberries and replacing them with the same quantity of raspberries.

sherry trifle smoothie
Prepare the basic recipe, adding 2 tablepoons sherry to the other ingredients before blending.

tropical fruit trifle smoothie
Prepare the basic recipe, omitting the strawberries and replacing them with 225 g (8 oz) mixed tropical fruit such as pineapple, mango, lychee and papaya.

fruit cocktail trifle smoothie
Prepare the basic recipe, omitting the strawberries and replacing them with the same quantity of tinned fruit cocktail.

chocolate trifle smoothie
Prepare the basic recipe, omitting the strawberries and ice cream, and replacing them with 2 tablespoons chocolate sauce and chocolate ice cream.

banana, cream and chocolate smoothie

see base recipe page 243

banana, cream and chocolate peanut smoothie
Prepare the basic recipe, omitting the grated chocolate and replacing it with
35 g (1¼ oz) chocolate-coated peanuts.

banana, chocolate cream and chocolate peanut smoothie
Prepare the basic recipe, omitting the grated chocolate and replacing it with
35 g (1¼ oz) chocolate-coated peanuts. Replace the vanilla ice cream with
chocolate ice cream.

banana and chocolate smoothie
Prepare the basic recipe, omitting the vanilla ice cream and replacing it with
the same quantity of chocolate ice cream.

banana, caramel and chocolate smoothie
Prepare the basic recipe, omitting the vanilla ice cream and replacing it with
the same quantity of caramel ice cream.

ginger and pear pudding smoothie

see base recipe page 244

rich ginger and pear pudding smoothie
Prepare the basic recipe, adding 1 teaspoon black treacle to the other
ingredients before blending.

boozy ginger and pear pudding smoothie
Prepare the basic recipe, adding 2 tablespoons Poire William to the other
ingredients before blending.

rhubarb and ginger pudding smoothie
Prepare the basic recipe, omitting the pear and replacing it with 115 g (4 oz)
stewed rhubarb.

pear and rhubarb smoothie
Prepare the basic recipe, omitting the ginger ice cream and replacing it with
vanilla ice cream and adding 115 g (4 oz) stewed rhubarb. Swap the ginger
biscuits for oatmeal biscuits.

apple crumble smoothie

see base recipe page 247

mulled apple crumble smoothie
Prepare the basic recipe, omitting the cinnamon and replacing it with
1 teaspoon mixed spice and 2 tablespoons Calvados.

apple and blackberry crumble smoothie
Prepare the basic recipe, adding 60 g (2¼ oz) stewed blackberries to the
other ingredients before blending.

apple and rhubarb crumble smoothie
Prepare the basic recipe, adding 60 g (2¼ oz) stewed rhubarb to the other
ingredients before blending.

rhubarb crumble smoothie
Prepare the basic recipe, omitting the stewed apples and replacing them
with the same quantity of stewed rhubarb.

boozy blends

For a more grown-up taste, try adding an alcoholic kick to your blended drinks. Sit back and enjoy the drinks in this chapter – perfect for parties or to help you relax in the evening.

watermelon martini

see variations page 274

A light and refreshing drink, ideal to serve as an ice-breaker at the start of a party.

225 g (8 oz) peeled watermelon chunks
6 ice cubes
2 tbsp vodka
1 tbsp sugar syrup (page 12)
2 tsp vermouth
2 fresh mint leaves
Slice of watermelon to serve

Put the watermelon through a juice extractor. Place into a cocktail shaker with the ice, vodka, sugar syrup, vermouth and mint, and shake vigorously for 30 seconds. Pour through a strainer into a martini glass and serve with a slice of watermelon.

Serves 1

passion fruit margarita

see variations page 275

Despite the small quantity of juice that can be obtained from a passion fruit, its astringent flavour and tropical perfume permeate this drink.

Juice of 6 passion fruit, sieved
6 ice cubes
2 tbsp tequila
2 tsp triple sec
1 tbsp sugar syrup (page 12)

Put the passion fruit juice, ice, tequila, triple sec, sugar syrup and mint into a cocktail shaker and shake vigorously for 30 seconds. Pour through a strainer into a martini glass. Garnish with a passion fruit half if desired.

Serves 1

piña colada

see variations page 276

Although this classic cocktail has been the subject of lighthearted songs, its intense Caribbean flavours deserve to be taken seriously.

225 g (8 oz) peeled pineapple chunks
60 ml (2 fl oz) coconut milk
60 ml (2 fl oz) white rum
1 glassful ice cubes
Sparkling water
Slice of pineapple to serve
Maraschino cherries to serve

Put the pineapple through a juice extractor. Pour into a blender along with the coconut milk, rum and ice. Blend for 1 minute. Pour into a tall glass or goblet. Top off with a splash of sparkling water. Serve with a slice of pineapple and a couple of maraschino cherries.

Serves 1

amaretto and apricot boozy smoothie

see variations page 277

The Italian combination of apricot and almond makes for a stylish adult-friendly smoothie – especially when the almond flavour comes from amaretto liqueur.

4 very ripe apricots, stoned
60 ml (2 fl oz) Disaronno amaretto liqueur
60 ml (2 fl oz) orange juice
120 ml (4 fl oz) plain low-fat yoghurt
2 amaretto biscuits, crumbled, to serve

Place the stoned apricots, amaretto liqueur, orange juice and yoghurt into a blender. Blend for 1 minute or until smooth. Pour into a glass and serve with the crumbled biscuits on top.

Serves 1

clementine and mango mojito

see variations page 278

This exotic cocktail is much improved by the addition of the clean, crisp flavour of fresh mint.

55 g (1³/₄ oz) peeled mango chunks
1 peeled clementine, cut into eighths
1 tbsp white rum
1 tsp brown sugar
Small handful fresh mint leaves
Ice cubes
Sparkling water

Put the mango through a juice extractor and pass through. Place the clementine pieces into a tall glass with the brown sugar and mint and, with a muddler or spoon handle, crush together to release the flavours. Add the mango juice and white rum and mix thoroughly. Stir in some ice cubes until they reach the top of the glass. Top with sparkling water. Garnish with a fresh mint sprig if desired.

Serves 1

strawberry frozen daiquiri

see variations page 279

This cool red liquid is sipped through ice crystals and looks stunningly vibrant.

200 g (7 oz) strawberries, hulled
Squeeze of lime
1 tbsp sugar syrup (page 12)
1 glassful ice cubes
1 tbsp white rum

Place all the ingredients into a blender and blend until slushy. Pour into a glass and serve immediately.

Serves 1

fruity gin fizz

see variations page 280

A light and fragrant drink made all the more glamorous with a dash of sparkling wine.

75 g (2³/₄ oz) peeled and stoned lychees
175 g (6 oz) seedless grapes
1 tbsp elderflower cordial
1 tbsp gin
Ice cubes
Sparkling wine or champagne to serve

Put the lychees and grapes through a juice extractor. Pour into a cocktail shaker along with the elderflower cordial and gin. Shake vigorously for 30 seconds. Pour into a glass over ice and top off with the sparkling wine or champagne.

Serves 1

papaya and orange rum slush

see variations page 281

The soft, sweet flesh of a papaya is the perfect foil for the acidic hit of orange juice, and the ice cubes make this drink particularly good in the summer months.

1 papaya, peeled and deseeded
60 ml (2 fl oz) orange juice
Juice of 1 lime
1 tsp brown sugar
1 tbsp brown rum
1 glassful ice cubes

Place all the ingredients into a blender. Blend for 1 minute or until slushy. Pour into a glass and serve immediately.

Serves 1

bloody mary

see variations page 282

The great classic, slightly remodeled into a lighter drink. It will certainly refresh you, but it will not make you lose your appetite in the way a standard Bloody Mary does.

6 tomatoes
$1/2$ lemon, peeled
2 tbsp vodka
Pinch salt
Pinch celery salt, plus more to serve
Ground black pepper, plus more to serve
1 tbsp Worcestershire sauce
Dash Tabasco sauce
Ice cubes to serve
1 stalk celery, trimmed

Put the tomatoes and lemon through a juice extractor. Place in a cocktail shaker with the vodka, salts, pepper, Worcestershire sauce and Tabasco. Shake vigorously for 30 seconds. Pour into a tall glass over ice. Top with some more celery salt and pepper. Serve with a stalk of celery.

Serves 1

rum and raisin ice cream milkshake

see variations page 283

This shake is rich and exotic, but not as heavy as plain ice cream.

35 g (1¼ oz) raisins
60 ml (2 fl oz) dark rum
1 tbsp brown sugar
300 ml (10 fl oz) vanilla ice cream
2 tbsp milk

Mix the raisins with the rum and sugar, and leave to soak overnight. Place in a blender with the vanilla ice cream and milk. Blend for 1 minute or until smooth. Pour into a glass and serve immediately.

Serves 1

variations

watermelon martini

see base recipe page 257

pineapple martini
Prepare the basic recipe, omitting the watermelon and replacing it with 450 g (1 lb) peeled and chunked pineapple.

appletini
Prepare the basic recipe, omitting the watermelon and replacing it with 2 peeled and cored apples.

green appletini
Prepare the basic recipe, omitting the watermelon and replacing it with 2 peeled and cored apples. Add 1 tablespoon Midori.

strawberry martini
Prepare the basic recipe, omitting the watermelon and replacing it with 150 g (5½ oz) hulled strawberries.

mango martini
Prepare the basic recipe, omitting the watermelon and replacing it with 225 g (8 oz) peeled and chunked mango.

variations

passion fruit margarita

see base recipe page 258

lime margarita
Prepare the basic recipe, omitting the passion fruit juice and replacing it with 2 tablespoons lime juice.

lemon margarita
Prepare the basic recipe, omitting the passion fruit juice and replacing it with 2 tablespoons lemon juice.

grapefruit margarita
Prepare the basic recipe, omitting the passion fruit juice and replacing it with the juice of ½ grapefruit.

mandarin margarita
Prepare the basic recipe, omitting the passion fruit juice and replacing it with the juice of 1 mandarin orange.

variations

piña colada

see base recipe page 261

banana colada
Prepare the basic recipe, omitting the pineapple and replacing it with 1½ peeled and chopped bananas.

mango colada
Prepare the basic recipe, omitting the pineapple and replacing it with 225 g (8 oz) peeled and chunked mango.

papaya colada
Prepare the basic recipe, omitting the pineapple and replacing it with 225 g (8 oz) peeled and chunked papaya.

strawberry colada
Prepare the basic recipe, omitting the pineapple and replacing it with 150 g (5½ oz) hulled strawberries.

piña chi chi
Prepare the basic recipe, substituting an equal amount of vodka for rum.

amaretto and apricot boozy smoothie

see base recipe page 262

amaretto and plum boozy smoothie
Prepare the basic recipe, omitting the apricots and replacing them with
4 very ripe plums, stoned.

amaretto and prune boozy smoothie
Prepare the basic recipe, omitting the apricots. Replace them with 6 prunes
that have been stoned and soaked for 30 minutes in 3 tablespoons of
hot water.

amaretto, apricot and plum boozy smoothie
Prepare the basic recipe, omitting 2 of the apricots and replacing them with
2 very ripe plums, stoned.

amaretto and cherry boozy smoothie
Prepare the basic recipe, omitting the apricots and replacing them with
200 g (7 oz) tinned cherries.

clementine and mango mojito

see base recipe page 265

mojito
Prepare the basic recipe, omitting the clementine and mango, and replacing them with 2 peeled and chopped limes.

berry mojito
Prepare the basic recipe, omitting the clementine and mango, and replacing them with 1 peeled and chopped lime and 35 g (1¼ oz) mixed berries.

lime and strawberry mojito
Prepare the basic recipe, omitting the clementine and mango, and replacing them with 1 peeled and chopped lime and 35 g (1¼ oz) hulled strawberries.

lemon mojito
Prepare the basic recipe, omitting the clementine and mango, and replacing them with 1 peeled and chopped lemon.

pineapple mojito
Prepare the basic recipe, omitting the clementine and mango, and replacing them with 225 g (8 oz) peeled and chopped fresh pineapple.

strawberry frozen daiquiri

see base recipe page 266

raspberry frozen daiquiri
Prepare the basic recipe, omitting the strawberries and replacing them with the same quantity of raspberries.

watermelon frozen daiquiri
Prepare the basic recipe, omitting the strawberries and replacing them with the same quantity of chopped watermelon.

mango frozen daiquiri
Prepare the basic recipe, omitting the strawberries and replacing them with 225 g (8 oz) peeled and chunked mango.

pineapple frozen daiquiri
Prepare the basic recipe, omitting the strawberries and replacing them with 225 g (8 oz) peeled and chunked pineapple.

variations

fruity gin fizz

see base recipe page 267

redcurrant, elderflower and lychee gin fizz
Prepare the basic recipe, omitting the grapes and replacing them with
150 g (5½ oz) redcurrants. Serve with a few loose redcurrants.

strawberry, elderflower and lychee gin fizz
Prepare the basic recipe, omitting the grapes and replacing them with
150 g (5½ oz) hulled strawberries.

blueberry, elderflower and lychee gin fizz
Prepare the basic recipe, omitting the grapes and replacing them with
150 g (5½ oz) blueberries.

raspberry, elderflower and lychee gin fizz
Prepare the basic recipe, omitting the grapes and replacing them with
150 g (5½ oz) raspberries.

papaya and orange rum slush

see base recipe page 269

papaya and orange vodka slush
Prepare the basic recipe, omitting the rum and replacing it with the same quantity of vodka.

papaya and orange bourbon slush
Prepare the basic recipe, omitting the rum and replacing it with the same quantity of bourbon.

mango and orange rum slush
Prepare the basic recipe, omitting the papaya and replacing it with 115 g (4 oz) peeled and chopped mango.

pineapple and orange rum slush
Prepare the basic recipe, omitting the papaya and replacing it with 115 g (4 oz) peeled and chopped pineapple.

variations

bloody mary

see base recipe page 270

mexican bloody mary
Prepare the basic recipe, omitting the lemon, celery salt, Worcestershire sauce and Tabasco. Replace them with the same quantities of lime, cumin, coriander leaves and jalapeño Tabasco. Omit the celery stalk and replace it with a slice of avocado.

japanese bloody mary
Prepare the basic recipe, omitting the lemon, celery salt, Worcestershire sauce and Tabasco. Replace them with the same quantities of lime, wasabi, soy sauce and nanami togarashi seasoning. Omit the celery stalk and replace it with a slice of avocado.

virgin mary
Prepare the basic recipe, omitting the vodka.

bull shot
Prepare the basic recipe, omitting the tomatoes and celery stalk, and replacing them with 480 ml (16 fl oz) hot beef stock.

rum and raisin ice cream milkshake

see base recipe page 273

rum and prune ice cream milkshake
Prepare the basic recipe, omitting the raisins and replacing them with
45 g (1½ oz) stoned prunes.

rum, prune and chocolate ice cream milkshake
Prepare the basic recipe, omitting the vanilla ice cream and replacing it with
the same quantity of chocolate ice cream.

rum and tropical fruit ice cream milkshake
Prepare the basic recipe, omitting the raisins and replacing them with the
same quantity of mixed dried tropical fruits.

minced pie ice cream milkshake
Prepare the basic recipe, but replace the raisins with the same quantity of
mixed dried fruit and citrus peel, soaked in brandy rather than rum.

index

recipes

ingredients